PRAISE FO

Employees First!

"Donna Cutting's new book is filled with compelling stories, actionable strategies, and tremendous heart. *Employees First!* will help you build a winning service culture with inspired team members who serve better, care more, and love life!"

—Ron Kaufman, *New York Times* bestselling
author of *Uplifting Service*

"*Employees First!* is a must-read for anyone running an organization. Cutting has done an incredible job outlining what it takes to create a culture where your employees feel valued and, as a result, are more engaged and excited about the work they are doing with your company. It's an easy read with practical advice that will absolutely get you thinking about how to improve your company."

—JJ Ramberg, cofounder, Goodpods and
former anchor, MSNBC's *Your Business*

"You can't deliver *amazing* service unless your employees are feeling the love. With *Employees First!,* Donna Cutting gets real about creating a culture that inspires your people to want to give the best service to your customers."

—Shep Hyken, customer service/experience expert and
New York Times bestselling author of *The Amazement Revolution*

"I *love* this book! Using current research and real-life stories, Donna has powerfully advocated for the desperate need to address the *human* aspect of service. Both employees and customers are served best when feelings, empathy, empowerment, and appreciation are present along with necessary policies and procedures. In order to be successful in this post-pandemic culture, every leader should read and apply the ideas and principles in this book."

—Barbara Glanz, Hall of Fame speaker and author of
The Simple Truths of Service: Inspired by Johnny the Bagger
and *Care Packages for the Workplace*

"Donna Cutting's *Employees First!* is authentic, powerful, and relatable. In this must-read, she tells a story of experience, empowerment, and leadership that will resonate with you as we navigate a pandemic and the many shifts that now exist in the workplace. There couldn't be a better time for this book to hit the shelf!"

—Dr. Simon T. Bailey, executive coach,
author, and thought leader

"Donna Cutting shines new light on the connection between happy employees and a healthy bottom line. Through inspiring stories and real-world examples, she creates a practical path for leaders to maximize the experience for employees and customers alike. Apply the prescriptive advice in these pages to fuel the growth of your people and your organization!"

—Richard Hadden, CSP, employee engagement speaker,
coauthor, *Contented Cows STILL Give Better Milk*

"Donna has done it yet again, another masterpiece on the importance of customer service but this time as it relates to your employees. Her message could not be more relevant with the workforce crisis employers find themselves in. Read this book, execute upon it, and make employees the heart of your organization rather than its Achilles heel!"

—Traci Bild, CEO, Bild & Co and
author of *Zero Lost Revenue Days*

EMPLOYEES FIRST!

*Inspire, Engage, and Focus
on the
Heart of Your Organization*

DONNA CUTTING

Foreword by
JEFFREY W. HAYZLETT

CAREER
PRESS

This edition first published in 2022 by Career Press, an imprint of
Red Wheel/Weiser, LLC

With offices at:
65 Parker Street, Suite 7
Newburyport, MA 01950
www.careerpress.com
www.redwheelweiser.com

ISBN: 978-1-63265-200-3

Library of Congress Cataloging-in-Publication Data available upon request.

Cover design by Kathryn Sky-Peck
Interior by Timm Bryson, em em design, LLC
Typeset in Adobe Garamond Pro

Printed in the United States of America
IBI

10 9 8 7 6 5 4 3 2 1

TO

Lucy Bosy, Mary E. Collazo, Rachel Street,
Michelle Merger, Katie Locke, David Mendes,
Chris Perillo, Julie Read, Beth Johnson, Brandi Hand,
Linda Wright, Raj Anderson, Connie Portman,
and all who have contributed to the mission and
message of The Red-Carpet Way!

CONTENTS

FOREWORD

It's always about the people! They are the engines that make businesses run and any organization's most valuable asset. Treating people well isn't a new, or novel, concept. It shouldn't be, at least. Much focus has been placed on profits, spreadsheets, corporate boards, and shareholders. Often people have been sacrificed to the altar of profits, but the shift in corporate culture in recent years has made everyone pivot . . . and rightfully so.

People over profits—it's that simple.

However, where's the red carpet for our own workers? Those who ensure that the leadership team hits their mark, things run smoothly, and everything is executed flawlessly? The people behind the scenes are the unsung heroes of every organization.

It's critical for every organization to inject "humanity" into the workforce. Right from the onboarding process, your employees need to feel like they matter, that what they're doing matters, and that they're helping move the needle forward. However, they won't know unless you tell them.

Leaders need to remember that it's their people who will eventually become their brand ambassadors. They're the ones who will live the company's mission, vision, and values and those who will evangelize the brand internally and externally.

When employees feel appreciated, they become your constants. With so many changes happening in today's world, executive leaders need to rely on their true norths to carry them through difficult times. "You reap what you sow" is more than just a common adage, it's something everyone should live by. You provide a red-carpet treatment for your employees and they'll reward you with their effort, time, and loyalty.

There's no longer a clear distinction between the professional and personal. It's all blended together, and the sooner we recognize that we can't use silver bullets to fix employee retention issues, the better for our businesses.

With this book, Donna has taken a slightly different approach, shining the spotlight on another group: those who make customer service happen. With business moving at warp speed, the workplace has transcended beyond leaders having the solution to every problem. Power has been decentralized and it's on every leader to empower every employee to find the answers and even help leaders figure out a solution that's beneficial to all.

—Jeffrey W. Hayzlett, primetime TV and podcast host; chairman and CEO, C-Suite Network; keynote speaker; and bestselling author

INTRODUCTION

There couldn't be a better time to reimagine the employee experience. Face it. What you've tried hasn't worked. The recognition programs, the pizza parties, the surveys, and the suggestion boxes have not helped you retain employees. They are tactics that amount to tap dancing around the real problem. You're not going to resolve turnover with a program. You'll find the solution in your culture. It's about how your people feel in their relationships with their boss or their coworkers. It's about whether they truly feel listened to and included. It's about feeling connected to a purpose rather than a paycheck (although that paycheck also comes into play). It's about feeling like there's time to do what truly matters, and it's feeling like you (their employer/boss) care about them.

Notice the use of the word *feeling?* That's intentional. Once, after hearing one of my presentations, a man said what he liked about my approach was that I spoke to the *emotions* behind employee and customer experience, rather than listing a bunch of facts and strategic initiatives. I had never thought of it like that until he articulated it, but of course! It's *all* about emotions!! Whether it's customers or coworkers, it's *all* about the way you make them *feel*.

The need to put employees first is not a new idea. The model known as the *Customer-Service-Profit Chain*[1] is the theory that when you treat your employees well, they will treat your customers well. Your company will become more financially successful as a result. The 2020 HR Sentiment Study, conducted by Future Workplace in the first quarter of 2020[2], asked human resource professionals and business leaders what their top initiatives for the year would be. More than 50 percent ranked a focus on the employee experience first. Chances are you've been talking about employee retention and engagement for a while now. You've rolled out initiatives. You've surveyed your employees and pored over results trying to figure out what will make them stay. You've held appreciation events and created elaborate recognition programs. Has it worked? Probably not. According to the 2019 Retention Report conducted by the Work Institute, there has been an 88 percent increase in US employee turnover since 2010, and the global talent shortage in April 2020 was almost double what it was ten years prior.[3] With all the focus on employee retention and engagement strategies, the numbers have been getting worse, not better.

Then, in early 2020, we were hit by a worldwide pandemic that changed everything. Employees were laid off, or furloughed, or sent to work from home—except, of course, those deemed *essential,* who put their safety at risk to take care of the needs of others. While we all hoped we'd go back to normal in three to six weeks max, as I write this book it's been a year, and we are only now beginning to roll out the vaccines we hope will save us. The US unemployment rate is double what it was in February 2020, before COVID-19 hit the country. People are re-evaluating their work-life-balance and are leaving their jobs in what the media deems "the great resignation." The total impact on the United States and the global economy is yet unknown. The workplace has undoubtedly changed, and, I must admit, it's daunting to write a book about the employee experience in a time of such incredible, evolving transformation. While the future of work remains to be seen, many experts agree on the following:

- People will continue to work remotely or enjoy a hybrid experience, heading into the office a few times a week but working from home (or elsewhere) more often than before.
- There will be a greater focus on wellness, safety, and mental health in the workplace.
- We'll pay greater attention to diversity, equity, and inclusion.
- Leaders will be purposeful with transparent communication and looking for ways to keep virtual and "on-location" employees connected.

Moreover, our priorities have shifted. People are re-evaluating their work requirements and looking for flexibility to spend more time nurturing relationships, having work-life balance, and enjoying interests outside of their jobs.

If 2020 taught us anything, it's that we cannot separate our human selves from our work selves. We left behind the attitude of "leave your problems at the door," as employees coped with working from home while homeschooling children, dramatically reduced income because one spouse or partner lost their job, and fear of becoming ill or even dying due to social interactions. We began to embrace humanity at work, and it's essential we continue.

If you're expecting this book to provide a magic bullet to solve your turnover problems, you'll be disappointed. However, if you want to get to the heart of the matter, and build a culture where your people feel respected, included, and excited to go to work in your organization, then you're in the right place.

You'll enjoy the stories of people in various organizations, such as a baseball team that goes bananas, a digital marketing company with an entirely remote workforce, and two senior living organizations dedicated to more diverse, equitable, and inclusive practices. You'll read about leaders in a technology company who are obsessed with transparent communication, a university hotel where the approach to safety is all about empowerment, and a bank with team members who are intentional about kindness. You'll benefit from the dozens of interviews I held with experts and leaders in a variety of fields who are working toward a better employee experience. Unless otherwise cited, all quoted material in this book comes directly from those conversations.

You will learn how to give your people a purpose they care about, how to create a culture of curiosity and respect, and how to roll out the red carpet for an employee's first day! You'll get new ideas for communicating with your team, keeping your remote team connected, and building a culture where everyone feels welcome. You'll hear from a group of hourly employees about what truly makes them feel valued. (It may not be what you think!) You'll dive into the topics of wellness, mental health, and safety. There's even a chapter on employee compensation. (Oh, yes. We're going there.)

I hope that by the end of this book, you'll be ready to let go of your quick-fix approach to employee turnover and start having conversations about creating a culture that makes people want to come to work. A culture that prioritizes respect, care, and inclusiveness, and lets your team members know how much they matter. It's time to move out of our heads and into our hearts.

Are you ready? Let's get started!

CHAPTER ONE

Give Them Something to Care About

Jesse Cole is a man on a mission. He has more enthusiasm than a stadium full of cheerleaders and enough energy to power the city of, well, Savannah, Georgia. He first came to my attention through a handwritten note he sent to thank me for writing *501 Ways to Roll Out the Red Carpet for Your Customers*. Knowing Jesse now, I suspect I am not the only author who has received such a note, but, as you can imagine, it made my day! One quick search on Google, and I soon learned that Jesse Cole is no ordinary fan. Images of a young man wearing a bright yellow tux and hat and dancing in the stands at a baseball game leaped out at me from my browser—photos of Jesse himself. Videos of sunshine-yellow-clad baseball players juggling, dancing, and passing the ball between each other neck-to-neck. Grandmothers line dancing on the field and children throwing banana cream pies into faces of the players. There was even an audacious video in which Jesse and his team offered newly out-of-office President Obama an internship with their company. *Who is this guy?* I thought to myself.

Jesse is the owner of Fans First Entertainment, the company that owns the Savannah Bananas, a Coastal Plain League team based at Grayson Stadium in Savannah, Georgia, and the most outrageous baseball team on the planet. Their mission is Fans First, Entertain Always, and people come from all over the country to see them play. By *play*, I mean both the game of baseball and party like it's 1999. They are 100-percent committed to creating a highly entertaining experience for the fans in the stands, and they aren't afraid to look a little outlandish doing it. Don't delay getting your tickets. Their games always sell out quickly.

It wasn't always like this. As Jesse puts it, *"In the early days, the struggle was real. In the first three months, we sold two tickets and received phone calls about our over-drafted account. My wife, Emily, and I sold our house and emptied our savings account to make payroll."* Today their stadiums are full every season, they've begun streaming their games to a select group of Bananas Insiders, and they have plans to play year-round, to take their show on the road, and to welcome a global audience. You might say he is a marketing genius, a more ethical P.T. Barnum of sorts, and the kind of man who knows what it takes to attract the best kind of attention. I would say he is a man with a big reason to jump out of bed every morning and a leader dedicated to instilling the same sense of purpose in the people who work for him.

Fans First teammates (as they refer to their employees) are also raving fans of the company and willing to do almost anything to see the organization succeed. Case in point, Johnathan Walters, the current stadium operations coordinator, who has done everything for the Bananas from Parking Penguin (dressing up in a penguin costume and directing parking lot traffic in the Savannah heat) to bartending to seasonal work. Johnathan exclaims, *"I'm so passionate about this place. There's something so special here, and it was worth it to be involved in something so big!"*

There's a reason I called this chapter "Give Them Something to Care About." If you're going to create an experience that retains and engages your employees in today's world, you'll need to focus on more than just your profits. Now, before you roll your eyes and throw this book to the side, know that, as a business owner myself, I understand that money matters. However, you can't even keep most of your profits if you're spending them on the high cost of employee turnover. The Deloitte Millennial Survey released in January 2014 shared that millennials will comprise 75 percent of the global workforce by 2025.[1] A Gallup report called "How Millennials Want to Work and Live" found that 21 percent of millennials say they've changed jobs within the past year, more than three times the number of non-millennials who reported the same. In the same report, Jim Clifton, Chairman and CEO writes, *"Millennials don't just work for a paycheck. They want a purpose. Compensation must be fair, but it's no longer what drives them."*[2] A 2018 study called the *Employee Retention Report* by TINYpulse found that employees who believe their company has a higher purpose over money-making are 27 percent more likely to stay, but 43 percent of millennials feel like their company only cares about proceeds or profits.[3] The Deloitte survey mentioned above also found that *"Millennials believe companies should measure success in terms of more than just its financial performance with a focus on improving society among the most important things it should seek to achieve."*

You might also suspect, as I do, that as we move into a post-pandemic workplace, it will be more than just the millennial generation on a search for greater meaning in their work.

Many of us have spent 2020 re-evaluating everything from our finances to our health and how we spend our money and time, including how and where we work. If you want to engage people and keep them loyal to your organization longer, it's time to give them something real to care about. *"There are a lot of reasons,"* Jesse Cole argues, *"that people under thirty years of age leave jobs so often. Perhaps it's the desire to have new experiences, try out new opportunities, or perhaps it's a case of 'the grass is always greener.' However, maybe it's also because they don't know what's next for the company. Maybe they don't know where the company is going, so they don't know if they want to be part of it. Maybe they don't know if they want to be on that particular bus because they're thinking, 'Hey, we just did this. Are we going to do the same thing next year? Are we just going to sell more? Are we just going to try to make more money?' When you have a much bigger vision than yourself and larger than just making a few dollars, your team will be inspired and say, 'I'm jumping on board! I'm all in!'"*

In my experience, Jesse's thesis proves to be true. Ask your frontline team members what they love most about their job, and you can bet their answer won't be "We're making the company so much money! Woo hoo!!" Instead, when I've asked this question of our customers' team members, the answers have been more along the lines of "I love my coworkers," "I love our customers," or "I'm making a difference." True, some think of their job as just a way to earn a paycheck and find their purpose outside the workplace, but studies have shown that employees who find meaning in their work are more engaged. In the "2017 Meaning and Purpose at Work Report," conducted by BetterUp Labs, a survey of 2,285 American workers found that employees whose work feels meaningful work an extra hour per week, are absent less, and turn over less. They found that organizations gain more than $9,000 per worker in productivity and retention when their employees find purpose in their work. Perhaps even more surprising is their discovery that more than nine out of 10 employees are willing to trade a percentage of their lifetime earnings for greater meaning at work.

Leaders can help their people find their purpose by focusing on their impact on the world rather than only focusing on profits. If you were lucky enough to have a job in 2020, you might have found that the pandemic gave you purpose. Healthcare workers joined forces around the common goal of keeping people with COVID-19 alive and giving their patients the absolute best care, all while waiting for adequate supplies. Senior-living caregivers kept the focus on keeping their residents and coworkers safe while keeping them connected to loved ones during a time of extreme isolation. Grocery store employees teamed up to keep their stores stocked, safe, and staffed as customers rushed in to supply themselves with pantry staples, hand sanitizer, and toilet paper. Teachers and school staff have the shared purpose of keeping children educated and nurtured, all while relentlessly working on mastering virtual learning tools. Employers rallied to keep their companies afloat while having and showing a deeper appreciation for their frontline workers. The impact was profound on overall employee engagement. In May 2020, the Gallup organization found 38 percent[4] of US workers were actively engaged, enthusiastic, and committed to their work, the highest number they had ever tracked.

As for the Savannah Bananas, Jesse told the Bananas staff, *"Yes, times are uncertain, but what we've got to do now is rally. We're all entertainers and what people need now is fun and joy and hope. It's time to produce content for our fans that's filled with off-the-charts entertainment."* He then painted a picture of what it was going to be like for them at the end of the crisis: *"When we open the stadium for opening night, people are going to be lined up for hours before the game. They're not going to walk into the stadium. They're going to run inside. They're going to see each other, and they'll be smiling and laughing. They'll be so excited to be back together. Just before the game, we're going to open up the gate at center field, and one after another, ambulances are going to come onto the field and line up behind home plate. Nurses and doctors will get out of those ambulances and line the entire field, standing side-by-side with the players during the national anthem. We're not going to have one person sing the national anthem. We're going to have everyone sing it together, and it's going to be a moment you'll never forget. You're going to tell your grandchildren about it. You'll tell them that you were part of bringing this country back together, how this little town in Georgia came back from the pandemic, and you were a part of it. That's what we're working toward right now."*

In the middle of unprecedented uncertainty, Jesse gave his people a purpose. After painting this picture of the future, he asked them, *"What's one word to describe what you're feeling right now?"* The words came. *Inspired. Creative. Happy. Hungry. Healthy. Fun.*

"What is this?" Jesse thought happily. *"Is there anything going on in the world right now?"* The Fans First Entertainment team and the Savannah Bananas innovated as they never had before. They created incredibly entertaining video content for their fans. They launched *Bananas Insiders,* a streaming platform allowing them to bring games and entertainment to hundreds of members worldwide. Magic happens when you give the people in your organization a shared purpose to rally behind.

For the team at Fans First Entertainment, this was just the beginning. The Savannah Bananas were one of a handful of baseball teams in the United States to have a season. They played at Grayson Stadium with many precautions and fewer fans in the stands, resulting in zero COVID cases. They also used the time to better articulate their purpose. Jesse told his team, *"When we finish this season, let's have a clear path for our team to be invigorated, excited, and ready to rock-and-roll."* Guided by the book *The Vision Driven Leader* by Michael Hyatt (Baker Books, 2020), they crafted and articulated an eleven-page vision for 2025 that addresses everything from the teammates they want to attract, the benefits they wish to provide, to products, promotion, culture, and impact. The final page reads:

> Millions of people are searching for fun, joy, happiness, and belonging. Because of what we do, our fans find this when they Go Bananas. No matter their age, ethnicity, or background, our fans feel like they belong at our show. As soon as they walk into a Bananas Experience, they feel **transported to a world of fun.** They sing, they dance, they laugh together. Together, our fans don't take themselves too seriously. They let loose and **Go Bananas in every way.** We are their First Game. We are their summer vacation. We are their reconciliation. We are their birthday celebration. We are their engagement. We are their family reunion. We are here to celebrate and **bring people together.**

Inspiring, don't you think?

So, what's your company's purpose? Answer the following questions as a start.

- How does our product or service make a difference in the lives of others?
- What impact do we want to have on the world?
- How large do we want that impact to grow?
- Who do we want to work with, and how do we want to work together?
- What kind of experience do we want to create for our customers and team members?

Once you understand your purpose and have a vision, the next question is, how do you take those carefully crafted words on a piece of paper and bring them to life, instilling a deep sense of purpose in the minds and hearts of your people. Here are a few steps to consider.

- Check your own sense of purpose.
- Involve your people.
- Lead by example.
- Be selective.
- Promote your purpose.
- Share Stories Worth Celebrating™.

Let's go through each of these steps in the remaining pages of this chapter.

CHECK YOUR OWN SENSE OF PURPOSE

When asked, *"What advice would you give a leader who wants to instill a sense of purpose within his or her team?"* Jesse replied, *"It's a big question. The place to start is with yourself. Do you (the leader) have a purpose that you get excited about? One that gets you up in the morning? Something you're fired up about and that you believe in? If you have that, it's easier to get your team on board."* Good advice. Consider brands that have long been hailed as the best in customer and employee experience: Southwest Airlines, Disney, and Virgin Group all had (or have) visionary founders whose missions went beyond profits, focusing more on making the world a better place. Whether it's connecting people to what's important in their lives (Southwest Airlines) to entertain, inform, and inspire (Disney) to changing business for good (Virgin Group), it's the impact these leaders made on the world that drove them to jump out of bed every morning. What drives you? Tap into that, and you might just find the juice that will fuel your team's motivation.

After reading my first two books or hearing me speak, people often say to me, "You're so passionate about customer service." I smile and thank them. Are you ready for a dirty little secret? I'm not. My company, Red-Carpet Learning Worldwide, sells customer service training, yes, but customer service itself is not what gets my juices flowing. It's the idea of making people feel important, special, and happier than they were 10 seconds ago. Today that mission is articulated: *To have, create, and teach others to create intentional encounters that lift people up!* That's my mission in life, and it's Red Carpet's mission. We enact it by helping organizations with their culture, their people, and their customer service, but it's not our educational programs that drive me. It's the impact they make on others that gets me going.

Still, even leaders with a higher purpose can lose their way. A few years back, burdened with the financial stresses of running and growing a company, I made the mistake of trying to inspire my team with money. I set the company's financial goal, shared it with the team, and even bribed them with big bonuses if we achieved it. I asked each team member what they would buy or do with those bonuses once we got there. We never did. I had a wonderful group of people inspired by the happiness and transformation we brought to our customers but frustrated by the constant focus on numbers and profits. In the end, my laser focus on revenue goals only had painful results, and even while we had happy customers, I became extremely unfulfilled, anxious, and unhappy. The team could see it and feel it, and the fallout was one of my most significant learning opportunities. It's only recently that I have remembered that the profits show up when you get back to your purpose. That's not to say I ignore the numbers. Of course, being fiscally responsible and making a profit are vital parts of running any business, large or small. Even not-for-profits must watch their dollars and cents. However, my primary focus is on my purpose and the impact I'm making on the people we serve so that they can make a difference for the people they serve. It's working. Today, I'm once again excited to wake up and get to work, and I will lead the Red-Carpet team from this sense of mission going forward.

Perhaps you began your career with a deep sense of mission but lost it somewhere along the way. The first step in generating a sense of purpose for your employees is getting back in touch with your own.

INVOLVE YOUR PEOPLE

One of the critical steps that often gets missed when it comes to launching initiatives in the workplace is involving people at every level of the organization. The C-Suite, management, and the "home office" sometimes sit in their bubble and make pronouncements without even asking the very people those decisions affect. As part of the research for this book, I spoke with Chad Mackay, CEO of Fire and Vine Hospitality, based in the state of Washington, about the compensation model he implemented for servers who work for his company. (You'll read more about it and its success in a later chapter.) One of the reasons for its success is that when he knew he would have to develop a new way of compensating his servers that was sustainable for his business, Chad went directly to them. He pulled together several servers who had seniority in the company, and they worked together to come up with a plan. They had some requests of him, and he had expectations of them. The result was a model that was not only sustainable but that helped the organization continue to grow and become more attractive to prospective employees. Chad also spoke of a competitor who adopted a similar model that failed. *"The difference,"* he says, *"is that I did it* with *my servers. The other guy did it* to *his servers without involving them at all."*

The way to get buy-in from your team is to involve them every step of the way. We learned this at Red-Carpet Learning when we came up with a way to scale our curriculum inside the organizations that work with us. Some of our customers have large learning and development departments. Others do not. It's not cost-effective for those companies to hire our team to do all the educating, so we created a Train-the-Trainer model, developing people at all levels of the organization to facilitate their custom-built curriculum. We involve their people every step of the way. In our discovery process, we sit down with dozens of employees to ask them questions. Their answers help us get a pulse on what's going on in the organization as well as design their curriculum. If we're producing videos for the customer, we may hire an actor or two, but their people are the film stars. Then, through our Train-the-Trainer process, their front-line and back-of-the-house employees and a few managers become adept at leading groups of their peers through the curriculum. We designed it this way for scalability.

However, the result has been that the companies have built-in evangelists or champions who are enthusiastically spreading the message of red-carpet customer service to their coworkers. Real behavior change is seen "on the floor," and employee engagement increases. We've coached some of our customers to lead similar discovery sessions with their people, pulling focus groups together and asking for feedback. Our customers consistently tell us how eye-opening the process of simply listening to their employees is for them. What's your listening strategy? Do you have one beyond your annual employee satisfaction survey?

There's an excitement and engagement that happens when you listen to and involve your people. Frankly, when you pull your employees in like that, the results are more inspired and creative than when leadership only is making decisions in a bubble.

At the end of a listening session I conducted for a customer, one of the participants came up to me and said, *"You know, Donna, if nothing ever comes of this conversation today, you still made a difference. You asked for our opinions, and you listened to our answers, and no one ever does that here. So, thank you."* I'm happy to say the organizational leaders started to have their own listening sessions and made many positive changes. If you want your team to buy into your mission and vision and wholeheartedly work with purpose every day, then listen to what they have to say and involve them in your programs, projects, and decisions.

LEAD BY EXAMPLE

Years ago, I worked with an organization that had its corporate office right behind one of its many locations. I was spending time at that location and asked one of the employees what it was like to have the home office right there, expecting that she would tell me how intimidating it was. Instead, she said, *"You know, you'd think it would be nerve-wracking, but our leaders are so approachable and helpful that it's great!"* She then proceeded to tell me how a regional director was there recently helping to unclog a toilet, and the CEO visited once, saw her working on a project, and put his briefcase down to help her before heading into his meeting. *"That's the kind of leadership,"* she said, *"that makes you want to give your all."* Indeed, it is.

If you want to inspire your people to work with purpose, you must be willing to get in the trenches. The days of leading from the safety of your office are behind you. Be visible and let everyone on your team see how dedicated you are to the mission and vision. When asked about the secret sauce that keeps the Bananas team bought-in, Fans First director Marie Matzinger replied, *"I can only speak for myself, but it's something that's reflected from the top down. I've seen the way Emily and Jesse put us first. At least for me, it's been something that has built my loyalty towards what we're doing here. I mean, they sold their dream house to ensure they made payroll. Time and again, they have put their own dreams aside to make sure that we, as a team, are successful. Seeing that example, we are all willing to do what's best for the team and each other. We've laid our stakes in the ground and decided that we may not all be best friends, but we have each other's back no matter what."*

When asked the same question, former Parking Penguin and current stadium operations coordinator Johnathan Walters said, *"It's the way the leadership holds themselves. There are times when I know they are working harder than we are, but they are out there with smiles on their faces looking like they are having a great time! If you were to walk into our front office today, you could tell that everyone has the same sense of purpose. We love what we do here, and we all want to help this team grow to greater heights! I believe the game day staff (part-time employees) feel the same, and it's because of the way our leaders behave. Now that I have grown into a leadership position, I strive to be a role model in that way as well."*

If you want your team to work with purpose, you've got to be out there leading by example.

BE SELECTIVE

In *501 Ways to Roll Out the Red Carpet for Your Customers*, I wrote about Talent Plus, a consulting firm based in Lincoln, Nebraska, that works with organizations to help them select and develop people with the right gifts to enliven their brands. Cydney Koukol, EVP, communities for the company, said something to me years ago that I remember to this day: *"With every person you hire, your culture either gets better or worse."*

Hiring people who align with your mission, vision, and values is critical to creating an exceptional employee experience. You don't want to get your current team all pumped up and purposeful only to bring on half-hearted people who could care less. By doing so, you send a message that, while your mission and vision are good ideas, you won't commit enough to get the right people on the bus. All that gusto will soon be gone. Fans First director Marie Matzinger confided, *"In terms of our full-time team, we don't even talk to a prospective teammate until we've shared our vision. We give it to them to read and say, 'Okay, if this is something that truly excites you, reach back out to us.' That's the precursor for any application interview or conversation."*

Cydney Koukol shared three practical steps to ensure you're selecting people who share your passion and purpose:

1. Make sure everyone at the senior leadership level believes in your mission. Having a clear vision that every senior leader is behind 100 percent is imperative.
2. Benchmark your best. By this, she means study your best people, and you'll know exactly who and what you're aiming for.
3. Have a consistent methodology for selecting people and ensuring that everyone in a hiring role is 100-percent committed to that process.

If you want your team to believe in your mission, hire others who also believe in and are committed to your mission.

PROMOTE YOUR PURPOSE

Ask an audience of leaders if their organizations have a mission, vision, and set of core values; almost all will raise their hands. Ask if they know what they are; most will raise their hands. Ask, however, *"If I walked through one of your buildings today asking your employees what those core values are and how they apply to their specific role in the company, would they know how to answer?"* A few hands might go up. *"Without looking at the reminder cards you provided?"* Most hands go down.

Hours, days, weeks, and months are committed to coming up with the perfect words to articulate the kind of company you want to be. You roll out those oh-so-perfect words in a big to-do with great excitement. You make posters and cards. You produce videos and tell your employees: This is who we are now! Aren't you thrilled?

Then . . . crickets. It's rarely talked about again.

Unless you want it to stick. Purpose-driven leaders are always promoting their passion. It's got to become part of the daily language of your company. At team meetings, in your employee newsletter, at annual retreats, on video chats, and anywhere you are communicating with your employees. Talk about it on the career page of your website. Let your prospective employees see what impact they can make when they come to work for your company. That purpose should be front and center anywhere that people are interacting with your brand. Jesse Cole of Fans First Entertainment has been on hundreds of podcasts in the last few years, on which he has shared stories of the impact his Bananas team has on fans. *"More often than not,"* he said, *"it's for our team to hear those stories. My goal is to keep them inspired."* He read that Bob Iger, executive chairman and former CEO of The Walt Disney Company, wrote press releases to inspire his employees. He'd tell the world what was next for Disney because he wanted his people to hear it and be proud of what they were doing. Jesse reiterated, *"If you want purpose, you need your people to feel proud of what they're doing."*

Want a sneak peek at their 2025 vision? Simply visit SavannahBananas.com and head to the About page. *"We made it public before most companies would be ready to do so. It's going to hold us accountable to our team, our interns, and our fans."*

You've got to incorporate your purpose into everyday rituals that include your team members. For instance, the Bananas full-time and game-day team members meet for ten minutes before every single game. During that time, they give shout-outs to people caught living their core values and putting fans first. They continually ask questions during one-on-one meetings with the leadership team: *What are we doing to create the best experience for our team? What are we doing to create the best company culture? What are we doing to reach our chosen destination? What are we doing to create surprises for our people?*

Often, you roll out the exciting vision, and then everyone goes back to business as usual. You've been there. The flavor of the month syndrome. (Insert eye roll here.) You must keep checking in with yourselves. *Are we doing this? Are we leading by example? Do we recognize successes that relate to our reason for being? Are we challenging ourselves to be better today than we were yesterday?*

At the end of every game, the full-time staff get together and review the day. They share their Fans First stories, which brings me to the last step.

SHARE STORIES WORTH CELEBRATING™

Every single day your team members are creating amazing stories. They're making moments that matter for customers and coworkers. It's inspiring! Well, it's inspiring if people know about it. I've long beaten the drum of how important it is to share Stories Worth Celebrating with your employees and others. These are tangible examples of your team living out your core values and impacting the lives of your customers and each other. Lists, bullet points, and statistics all have their place. However, it's stories that touch our hearts and make us laugh or cry. Stories have an emotional impact that moves people to action. Stories are the living, breathing examples of the culture you want to establish, and the more you tell them, the more your team members will want to create them.

During the pandemic, the Savannah Bananas, as I mentioned before, did manage to have a successful and safe season. At one of the last games, a father of young children approached Jesse with tears in his eyes. He said, *"You guys saved my life."* Jesse asked him, *"What are you talking about?"* The man replied, *"I was going through a dark time, but the fact that you played a season, and people danced, sang, and I got to come to the games and just feel a part of something again . . . it made all the difference. You helped me get out of the bad place and start enjoying life again."*

Think back to the first few lines of the last page of the Savannah Bananas vision: *Millions of people are searching for fun, joy, happiness, and belonging. Because of what we do, our Fans find this when they Go Bananas.* The story of this father is the embodiment of that very statement. When you share stories that exemplify your stated purpose, it can lift your people out of their day-to-day and reinforce that their work does make a difference.

If you want to touch your people's emotional heartstrings and inspire them to create more moments that matter for your customers and each other, become obsessive about noticing, collecting, recording, and sharing those Stories Worth Celebrating!

THE LAST WORD ABOUT PURPOSE

Finally, a reminder that your employees aren't inspired by how much money the company makes or the profits that line the owner's pockets. They are more likely to be stirred into action by the impact they can make on the world and the difference they make in the lives of others. Life is short and, as I write this chapter, the world is in the middle of a collective values adjustment. People are re-evaluating their priorities, and since we spend a majority of our time at work, it's quite probable your employees will be looking for meaning in their day-to-day tasks. Don't wait for another crisis to give the people who work for you something to excite them. To earn your employees' enthusiasm, make them feel like they are part of something bigger than themselves. Your company's success will follow.

CHAPTER TWO

Show Them Authentic Appreciation

When you meet the team at Parkcrest Dental, the first thing that hits you is how friendly they are and how happy they seem. They also look like they're having fun! At least, that was my experience when I met them in a meeting room at their twice-annual staff team-building event. Like many of my customers do when I speak, they had rolled out a red carpet. This group, however, took it to a whole other level. A small group of T-shirt-clad dentists, dental assistants, dental hygienists, and administrative assistants flanked the carpet, carrying motivational signs, foam fingers, and noisemakers. As each person entered, they formed a human tunnel for attendees to walk through, shouting encouraging words and blowing celebration horns. The energy was off the charts!

They had decorated the room to the nines, and table tents identified where each team should sit. They weren't just any teams. They were Team Awesome, Team Rockstar, Team Model, Team Superstar, Team Shining Star, and Team OMG!!! I was to provide a full-day seminar on patient experience and customer service, but they held their typical monthly team meeting before my presentation. I sat to the side and watched as they gave updates, discussed core values, and read positive patient reviews aloud.

Then, Tiffani Killingsworth, Parkcrest Dental administrator, asked if anyone had any "lifesavers." Hands immediately went up, and she called on people. *"Joy was a lifesaver to me last week. Jimmy was sent home from school sick, and she took over my schedule so I could be with him."* Or *"I was running behind with patients one day. Kyle noticed, and without my even asking, he did Mrs. Bouchard's X-rays, so she didn't have to keep waiting. What a lifesaver!"* These coworker shoutouts went on for at least fifteen minutes and came accompanied with gifts! Colleagues shared lottery tickets, candy, gift cards, candles, and lotion, some of them presented in colorful gift bags and tissue paper. *"My gosh,"* I thought, *"these people really like each other."*

The lifesaver shout-outs have been happening at every monthly meeting since before Tiffani joined Parkcrest in 2012. It's a regular practice of coworkers showing appreciation for other coworkers for specific contributions. Sometimes someone will even thank an entire department. *"The gifts,"* explains Tiffani, *"were their idea! We never asked them to bring gifts for each other. They just started doing it as a thank you."*

In addition to monthly lifesavers, the team of seventy passes a "roving card" among each other. Tiffani shared, *"It's a simple Hallmark card with a message of thanks. The card is given to a person or a department for doing something above and beyond. Their name is written on the card. The next month, whoever has the card decides which person or department truly shined that month and passes the card along to them at our staff meeting. I think the one we have now has been going for about four years. Once it's filled up or getting ragged, we'll retire the card and start a new one."* Another fun device to inspire team members to acknowledge each other.

As I witnessed these exchanges, what struck me was not the gifts or the card or even the awards given during the event. It was how genuine they were and how much respect this team seemed to have for each other. As administrator, Tiffani also prioritizes finding ways to show gratitude for team members. For instance, in January 2021, she launched a 21 Days of Kindness campaign, gifting flower seeds to employees with the words *We're blooming with appreciation for you.* Just before the Super Bowl, she presented them with soup bowls that read, *"We think you're Soup-er."* She re-ignited their practice of Wow Wednesdays and provided notepads so team members could write little notes to each other. She filled 70 mason jars with flowers and left one on each person's desk with a bag of Reese's Pieces® and a message that read, *"We love you to pieces!"* Head to the dentist on Halloween, and you'll find them celebrating in full-themed attire, in everything from "Where's Waldo?" costumes to their much-loved Parkcrest Prom event.

Yes, they have fun, and Tiffani and her team always come up with creative ways to show they care about one another. However, it's not the costumes, the flowers, or the candy that provides the real magic. It's the intention behind it all. *"I'm constantly trying to come up with ways to brighten their day! We spend so much time here. Sometimes we spend more time with our coworkers than we do with our own families, so it's important that we respect each other, have fun, and treat each other as we would want to be treated,"* said Tiffani.

The proof is in the pudding. Employee turnover at Parkcrest Dental is low, and tenure is strong, with some who have been on the team for more than forty years. *"When people do leave,"* according to Tiffani, *"it's because they're retiring, or wanting to stay home with children, or because they're moving. If they leave for another job, they often want to come back and say they didn't realize how good they had it!"* A 4.8 rating by Parkcrest Dental patients on Google confirms the premise of this book! When you put your employees first and create a safe and happy environment for them, they will provide an outstanding experience for your customers.

When your employees feel genuinely appreciated for their contribution to your company, they are more likely to stay and be engaged. In a study conducted by Survey Monkey and the employee retention platform, Bonusly interviewed 1,500 employed Americans about their thoughts about recognition. Of those surveyed, 82 percent said they are happier when they feel recognized at work, 63 percent of the people who thought they were always or usually appreciated at work said they were unlikely to be seeking new employment in the following three to six months, and 43 percent of those who felt unrecognized were highly likely to be looking for a new job.[1] These statistics shouldn't surprise you. Numerous studies show that people want to feel appreciated by their bosses and their coworkers. Many also show that despite all the effort put into employee recognition programs, they are still not feeling the love!

The pins, the plaques, the pizza, the parties, and the parking spaces are ways to make the workplace fun, and they are excellent tools for recognition. They aren't, however, what make people feel appreciated. Having been there to witness the appreciation shown to team members by Parkcrest Dental doctors, bosses, and coworkers, I can attest to the fact that, while they love a good party, it's the genuine sentiment behind all the devices that make it a great place to work.

In reference to how employees, as a whole, are still not feeling valued, recognition guru Bob Nelson wrote the following in his book *1,001 Ways to Engage Employees: Help People Do Better What They Do Best* (Career Press, 2018):

> In my twenty-five years of working with this topic, I think it's because we often confuse the behavior of recognizing employees with the things that are associated with recognition (money, gift cards, points, pins, plaques, and so on).
>
> In fact, in my doctoral dissertation on the topic, I posed a simple question: Why do some managers use recognition while others do not? I found that a manager's access to tools, programs, or a budget for recognizing employees was not significant in causing them to actually recognize employees. Translation: Employees feel special from the act of being recognized in a timely, sincere, and specific way by someone they hold in high esteem when they do good work. This is why so many companies that spend millions of dollars on recognition tools, items, cash substitutes, and merchandise still often have a major portion of their employee population report that they don't feel valued.[2]

It's time to stop relying on the tools and start showing authentic appreciation for your employees. To help you understand what truly makes your people feel appreciated, I have some research of my own to share. Right now, my team and I are on a quest to interview a minimum of 250 hourly workers for a study we're calling "What Makes an Hourly Employee Feel Valued." We expect to publish the research by the time this book is released, and you can download a complimentary copy at *www.RedCarpetLearning.com/MakeMeFeelValued.*

In the meantime, here's a sneak peek into what we're hearing. We conduct the interviews over Zoom, and we're talking to people who work in various industries. The only criteria are that they earn an hourly wage and aren't in a management position. We're asking everyone the same eight questions. Here's an example of what we're learning.

1. Give me an example of a time when you felt genuinely valued at work.

> I took the initiative and did something on my own. I didn't do a song and dance about it, but it was noticed and appreciated. (They) came up to me and said, "Hey, that was genius! Great idea!"
>
> I feel that way every day here. The boss does not walk away without thanking us for what we have done. I feel very valued here, whereas, at any other job, it has not been that way.
>
> When I'm included, I feel valued. It's about the communication I receive and the projects they trust me with. For me, the trappings of Administrative Assistant's Day, giving you gifts or flowers, I like that less than when they ask me to help another department because I've succeeded in a particular area.

2. Give me an example of a time when you felt less than valued.

> I was on a group call, and one of my coworkers was very rude and going at me like an attack dog. I pushed back with facts and examples, but they kept at it. Management was on the call and afterward came up

to me, apologized, and said what this person did was not okay. But, at no point on the call did anyone say, 'We do not do that here. We do not treat people that way.'"

When you're working with salaried employees who are not pulling their weight.

I had a boss who, if I shared an idea, would say, "No, that's not a good plan." Then a few weeks later, she'd come back with the same idea and take full credit for it.

3. What is the best part of the job you're doing right now?

It's the little wins and making a difference. (For example) It's not grand, it's not fancy, it's not some high-end stock option, and it's not going to make the news to-night, but I know that (because of my work) forty families have bags of food for the holidays, and that is awesome for me. That is the best win in the world.

The best part of my current job is that my ideas are listened to, and I can affect change.

Working with my coworkers and customers and feeling like I made a difference.

4. In addition to financial compensation, what is the most important thing you look for in a job?

Recognition for a job well done and to be set up for success.

Professional memberships, education, and a chance for development.

Being underappreciated makes me want to leave a job. Feeling appreciated makes me want to stay.

Good communication and respect. Also, the resources I need to do a good job.

Work-life balance is crucial. I am willing to take a pay cut if I could have more work-life balance and time off.

5. There has been a trend in the business world to call employees (as a group) anything other than employees (associates, colleagues, team members, etc.). On a scale of 1 to 10, with 1 being not necessary and 10 being the most important thing ever, where would you rate that effort?

As I write this chapter, from fifty interviews, the average score is 2.8. Some find the language very important, but most, thus far, have said they couldn't care less. We'll see what the final tally is when we complete the study. In the meantime, regardless of what you call the people who work for you, remember that those types of gestures may be less important in terms of what truly makes them feel valued.

6. What do you wish managers/bosses would know about how to create a better employee experience?

Walk in your employees' shoes. Know every division inside and out so that you're coming from a place of knowledge when you are asking the hard questions.

Become more aware of ALL I do. Not just what's in my job description, but the million little things that do not get logged but are the more meaningful aspects of my day-to-day.

Do not be a manager behind the wall in the back of the store or the administrative area. Come out in front because I think people need to be reminded of all that the frontline people are facing every day.

Listen to your employees and if you're going to make a change, consider how it impacts them.

Communicate clearly and have our backs.

7. What makes you want to stay at a job? What makes you want to leave?

I want to leave when I'm being micromanaged. I want to stay when I feel like I'm appreciated and that I'm making a difference.

8. Think about the best boss you've ever had and tell me a story that illustrates why you think of them that way.

I worked at an (automobile and transmission repair company), and my boss said, 'Hey when you work on cars, I can sleep at night.' That made me feel really good, and it made me know that he believed in what I did and that I would get it right. I still live with that. I want you to be able to sleep at night whenever I touch anything, so I won't walk away from it until it is right.

He's very calm. Nothing ruffles him. One time I tried something new and messed it up badly. The department (who received the work) came back to my boss (upset). I realized my mistake, and my boss did not yell at me. Instead, we sat down, and he said, "Okay, let's see how we can fix it," and that was it.

That's a tiny sampling of the results we have thus far, but the comments are all pretty similar. People want to feel appreciated, be listened to and included, and feel like their bosses have their back. They want to be seen and heard, and they want clear communication and have what they need to be successful on the job. Almost without exception, when asked, "What's the best part of the job you're doing now?" the answers have focused on the people they work with and making a difference. Not one of our interview subjects thus far has said, "I feel most valued when I receive the most points in our company's recognition program." They haven't said, "I feel most valued because of our annual employee appreciation day." Nor have they said, "I feel most valued when they give us turkeys on Thanksgiving." Two or three people mentioned awards they had won, but it was the fact that their bosses nominated them and the kind words that went into the nominations that, according to our subjects, made them feel valued.

Don't get me wrong. I've been the "employee morale chairperson," and I love all the fun stuff! For people like me, it can make going to work something to look forward to every day. On the other hand, some people would rather do anything than attend another "forced-fun work function." So, yes, implement your programs and have your events, but be aware they may not be for everyone and don't use them as a substitute for what *truly* makes people feel valued. As you promote people into leadership positions, consider whether they have the natural ability and desire to show appreciation for their team members. Develop your leaders and future leaders to understand the importance of *authentic* appreciation and build the skills they need to make people feel respected. Tiffani Killingsworth is a great boss, not because she bought flowers for her team, but because she is the kind of leader who continually looks for ways to make people feel special. Devices like the lifesavers practice and the roving card simply reinforce the idea that respect and gratitude are essential parts of the Parkcrest Dental culture.

So, how do you change your mindset from recognition programs into one of authentic appreciation? Here are a few ideas.

NOTICE AND THANK THEM

Dawn Winder was one of the best bosses I ever had. At the time, I was an activities director at a continuing care retirement community where she was the executive director. One day, she called me into her office and told me she was worried about me. I didn't seem like myself, and she had noticed. I did what you never want to do in your boss' office. I cried. She listened as I unloaded all the stress I was feeling at the end of my rant said something along the lines of, *"I feel like I'm not getting anything accomplished!"* She addressed my overwhelm and helped me reprioritize. When I left her office, I felt better. It wasn't more than twenty minutes later that I noticed a card in my mail slot at the front desk. It had my name on it in Dawn's handwriting. Inside the card were photographs of me leading activities with our residents. The inscription read, *"Does this look like an activity director who isn't getting anything accomplished?"* She wrote that note more than two decades ago, and I still get choked up thinking about it, and I remember how good it felt that she noticed and valued what I was doing. She did this for others too. Dawn would often call us together to run outside and see the landscaping our maintenance and groundskeeping had done and encourage us to thank them. Or she'd show up with multi-colored sticky notes on which we would write inspiring messages of congratulations for one of our colleagues who had achieved something big.

Do you notice each person and what they bring to the team? Do you let them know? Use hand-written notes, sticky notes, gift cards, or online shout-outs. The most important thing to your employees is that you see who they are, what they bring to the table, and how their contribution matters. Encourage everyone on your team to notice each other's accomplishments and efforts as well, at team meetings, on your online communication channels, and in the company newsletter.

LISTEN TO THEM

When Steve Bonner was CEO of the Cancer Treatment Centers of America (CTCA), from July 1999 until the end of 2012, and then on the board for another two years, revenues grew from one million to more than three billion dollars. When he started, they employed approximately 280 people, and when he left, there were 5,500 CTCA team members working, primarily in five hospitals. He credits some of that success to their work, based on a book that came across his desk when he worked for McGraw Hill. Working with Michel Robert, the author of *Strategy Pure and Simple: How Winning CEOs Outthink Their Competition* (McGraw Hill, 1993), fifteen senior leaders created the first draft of their mission, vision, values, brand promise, and strategic driving force. Said Steve, *"Mike's theory is that there are ten driving forces that are present in every organization, but that there is only one you build your entire company around that sets you apart."* The leadership team decided that they were consumer-focused, making the patient experience their strategic driving force.

In some organizations, this would be the end of it. They'd roll the plan out to employees and expect them to jump on board. However, Steve understood that those 280 team members were the ones who worked directly with the patients and that it was their voice that mattered. He personally met with every single CTCA employee in groups, working 24 hours a day, including every shift. *"We shared the draft documents with them and rigorously captured their feedback. Then we'd refine the language and go back to them, seeking consensus. This effort endured in our culture because everybody owned it."*

It's important to note that Steve and his leadership team also listened to their customers. In fact, every single board meeting began with a patient sharing their experience. Says Steve, *"We linked customer satisfaction to the compensation program, including comprising 25 percent of the all employee annual incentive program. We used Net Promoter Score technology to measure patient delight. . . . and also used it to gauge employee delight. Bain audited our results and in a book on NPS, said that CTCA consistently achieved the highest NPS ratings of any company they had every studied."* These results happen when you listen to both customers and employees. To engage your people and get buy-in, you must involve them.

As we've already discussed, people are more connected to their work when they feel that they're making a real difference. Your employees are the closest people to your customers and the day-to-day. When you actively listen to them, you make them feel valued, and you gain critical information that can only make your company better.

BELIEVE IN THEM

When you trust your team members with important projects or invite their suggestions for improvements, this communicates how much you value them. Scott Norrell is the conference services manager and group reservations specialist at the Hotel at Auburn University and Dixon Conference Center. When I asked him about a time he felt genuinely valued at work, he told me one of many stories he said came to mind. *"Christmas,"* he said, *"is one of my favorite things ever, and the hotel is usually all decked out like the North Pole. I wondered what was going to happen with the decorations this year (due to the pandemic). Then the front office supervisor, Blaknie, received an email from our hotel manager asking us if we would like to handle the decorations since we would have to keep the project in-house."* The pair took on the task, and Scott, influenced by a family tradition, even invited regular guests to bring in ornaments, signed and dated, for the Auburn family tree. *"Seeing our team members walk in the next Monday when we had everything up seemed to lift everyone's spirits. You could tell that it mattered a lot to our coworkers and guests. What made me feel valued was the way everyone was so thankful, but also that our leadership team trusted us with something so important."*

Earl Williams also works for the Hotel at Auburn University as an Engineering Supervisor. He told me, *"My current boss, Renard Hatcher, is the best boss I've ever had. He has managed multiple four- and five-diamond hotels and is the one who hired me. After he interviewed me, we were sitting at the table, and he gave me that look like he believes in me. And guess what? That look never went away."* Then Earl pulled out a large binder to show me. It was a manual he created that contained everything he's learned about the building over the last five years. It's organized with tabs and accessible so everyone on the team can use it. *"Renard encouraged it. He could have said, 'Hey, I've been here for years, and you still have a lot to learn.' No. He allowed me to develop it, and it's such a reward seeing team members going to this book when they need to know something."*

People feel valued when you show them that you believe in them.

MENTOR THEM

You met Johnathan Walters in Chapter One. Remember the Savannah Bananas "Parking Penguin," who is now the stadium operations coordinator? In between those positions, he held jobs with the Bananas, including a seasonal one as director of concessions. His boss, also named Jonathan, was the person who built the team's food and beverage operation from the bottom up. When Jonathan Wood's wife was offered her dream job in another city, he knew he'd have to find the right person to take over his position. So, he began to teach Johnathan everything from flipping hamburgers to fixing hinges on the doors. Johnathan shared, *"I remember seeing his key chain with all the keys he had to keep track of and thinking, 'There's no way I could remember everything he has to remember!' To have someone like him care so much about my success was huge for me, and to be able to learn the entire food and beverage operation from the person who created it was amazing!"*

When I ask the people in my audiences to tell me about the best boss they ever had, it never fails that someone talks about the person who took them under their wing and mentored them. Are you a leader who looks for people to develop? Or are you a leader who feels threatened when others want to learn and grow? Great leaders want to bring others along with them. Start by noticing the strengths of the people on your team. Meet with them one-by-one and learn about their hopes, dreams, and goals. Rather than be the gatekeeper for all information, teach them as much as you can about the what, the why, and the how of your department, and mentor them in leadership skills. Be sure to be aware of your own biases and make sure you're offering guidance to a diverse group of people. Put concerns about losing your job or losing your employee aside. You'll have a stronger team and more loyal team members when you take an active role in encouraging their success.

INSPIRE AND DEVELOP THEM

When Dr. Nido Qubein was seventeen years old, he immigrated to the United States from the Middle East, with 50 dollars in his pocket and knowing very little English. Soon after that, he graduated with a bachelor's degree in human relations from High Point University in High Point, North Carolina, and a master of science in business education from the University of North Carolina in Greensboro. The highly successful businessman, author of eleven books, and professional speaker and consultant returned to High Point University in 2005 as president of the university. Since then, the private university has quadrupled its enrollment to a current total of 5,600 students. According to Roger Clodfelter, senior vice president for communications, they've gone from having seventy-five graduate students to a thousand graduate degree candidates and grown nine academic schools from three. When Nido started, the university's total revenue was 28 million dollars. It's now grown to $320 million in revenue. Their assets have grown from 56 million to 1.1 billion. The campus, which used to sit on 91 acres, now sits on 500 acres and students enroll from all fifty states and more than forty countries. In 2021 HPU was named, by *US News,* as the #1 Best Regional College in the South for the ninth consecutive year and #1 Innovative School in the same category for four straight years. HPU has also opened a $250 million Innovation Corridor devoted to STEM academic programs and research. And when it comes to preparing students for success, 97 percent of their graduates are employed or enrolled in graduate school within six months of graduating from HPU. That is eleven points higher than the national average! I featured them in my first two books, and each time I write a new one, I'm blown away by how they continue to grow.

Of the success, Nido (as I know him from the National Speaker's Association) stressed, *"It's an eco-system that you have to deliver in a congruent and consistent manner, and that eco-system has to have in it caring people who deliver appreciated service, and who believe in civility and kindness and stewardship and fellowship. Not because they're told to, but because it's who they are. Being comes before doing."*

Billed as the Premier Life Skills University®, High Point University's brand promise is that every student will receive an extraordinary education, in an inspiring environment, with caring people. To get the results, faculty and staff must deliver on that promise. It's not just the students, each of whom is assigned a success coach upon admission, who are inspired to be extraordinary. Dr. Qubein and his leadership team invest significant effort in challenging the staff to do the same.

"I need everyone here to believe in the cause and deliver on it every day." To that end, Nido is a featured speaker at all monthly staff meetings. *"I'm injecting concepts and ideas, trying to enlighten you and impress upon you how you can be excellent at what you do. I remind them that extraordinary is a choice. You can choose whether you want to be extraordinary and whether you want to be distinctive or commonplace. In making such choices, you determine your outcomes in life. Even the most gifted, the most skilled, the most talented, and the most intelligent human beings must be continually reminded what it takes to be really extraordinary."*

In addition to the monthly meetings, Nido provides seminars for his faculty and staff on communication skills, presentation skills, financial literacy, and other subjects to improve their lives. The HPU president admits he's a demanding boss. *"I lead my colleagues, hand-in-hand, side-by-side, and we march onwards and forwards. I explain the why and am open for disagreement and debate, but if you're not a good thinker, I will call you on it."* Nido and his leadership team have high expectations, and it's not for everyone. *"I'd be foolish to think that we make everyone happy."* However, for those who want the opportunity to hone their interpersonal and professional skills and be set up for great success, this is a place where you will grow and shine. Challenging your employees to become their best selves is a way to show that you believe in them and value what they bring to the table.

How can you use your own story to inspire the people who work for you? What can you offer them to help them grow, and learn, and become more successful? You may not have the motivational speaking skills of Nido, but you can find ways to show your appreciation by investing in your employees' personal and professional development.

With almost 2,000 employees, Nido can't speak to his employees every day, so he has identified what he calls his "levers" in the organization. He gives significant attention to coaching and guiding his leadership team, so they will do the same with their teams. He knows it starts at the top, however. *"I once coached the CEO of a multi-billion-dollar company who told me that his team was dysfunctional. Very quickly, I identified the problem. It was the CEO. He came in every day and screamed at his employees. Everything was about statistics and numbers. You've got to pay attention to how you treat people and the little things that make a big impact."*

For Nido and the leadership team at High Point University, that means coworker shoutouts at their monthly meetings, sending meals when someone is sick, flowers when they get married, and silver frames when a new baby arrives. It means wishing every employee a happy birthday! It also means challenging them to be extraordinary. *"The magic,"* says Nido, *"is in the mix!"*

FOUNDATION FIRST

You may think I'm asking you to toss the tools of recognition and fun at work. I'm not. I'm the first to say that I love a good movie theatre gift card and a workplace birthday brunch! However, don't mistake the tools for real gratitude. Use them to complement your culture of genuine appreciation and respect. Tiffani Killingsworth points to the Parkcrest Dental Culture Guide, which acts as a compass for their staff, encouraging them to "Be Nice!," "Acknowledge Each Other," and "Treat Each Other With Respect." She uses it, when necessary, to remind her teammates who they are and who they strive to be. They are the foundational principles of caring for coworkers and customers that set the stage for best practices like "lifesavers," "the roving card," and events like Parkcrest Prom. In other words, employee appreciation is more than a special occasion.

CHAPTER THREE

Cultivate a Culture
of Kindness and . . .

When you think of the word *banker,* a self-proclaimed former jazz musician and closeted actor, comedian, and performer, who talks about creating an organization where people treat each other lovingly, may not be what comes to mind. Yet, that describes Ron Green, president and CEO of Oregon Pacific Bank (OPB). He's not your typical banker. Headquartered in Florence, Oregon, the bank has more than 130 employees and serves five communities. Their mission is "Together we can make your future better, in a way that's anything but ordinary." When you dig a little on their website and social media channels, you get the feeling that they do operate from a sense of purpose, striving to make the lives of small business owners and the communities they serve, better. Moreover, they were founded in 1979 on the idea of a culture of kindness, and that, according to Ron, *"really drives everything we do."* He elaborated, *"We commit to creating value for our four pillars, which are, in no particular order, our clients, our employees, our shareholders, and our communities. When we talk about value, it means economic value, yes, but also societal value in terms of how people feel in relationship to you."*

The leadership at Oregon Pacific Bank puts their money where their mouth is when it comes to a culture of kindness. All non-exempt staff get forty-eight hours of paid leave every year to volunteer out in the community. Also, team members can wear jeans on Fridays in exchange for a $5 donation to charity. The employees take their kindness culture seriously as well. Ron related a call he received during the northwest fires in 2020. *"As the CEO of the bank, I don't often receive calls directly from our clients. When they do call me, it's usually because of a complaint. This time, I picked up a voicemail from a woman. We'll call her 'Mrs. Johnson.' She said, 'My name is Mrs. Johnson, and I really need to speak to you. Here's my number.' Click. Oh, great,"* thought Ron. *"So, I call her, and even before she gets her words out, I can hear how emotional she is."* It turns out that Mrs. Johnson had a ranch right in the middle of the Oregon fires, with livestock and the works. She lost everything and was just trying to evacuate her family and her animals to safety. One of the bank employees offered her property for Mrs. Johnson to store her trailer and surviving animals for as long as needed. *"One of our people,"* said Ron, *"saw a need and felt empowered to make a choice to do what she felt was the right thing. I agreed with her. It made a huge impact on our client that her banker would take a personal interest and help her in this way during their time of need."* While he respects the line that must exist in professional relationships with your clients, Ron said, *"It's important that our employees know that they can treat our clients in a loving way and help them sometimes outside of the banking environment."*

Ellen Huntingdon, the marketing manager for OPB, concurs and adds that their culture of kindness begins at home. *"It's so inspiring to see management step up and be concerned about their employees as human beings. One of our branch managers reached out about one of her team members evacuating their home. Everyone automatically banded together to make sure he had a place to stay, food, and clothing. Without a second thought (my coworkers) stepped up, offering to take him to lunch, to dinner, and to provide clothing. It was just inspiring."*

Inspiring, indeed! Creating a culture of kindness, however, means more than empowering charitable acts. *"It starts,"* said Ron, *"with true common sense with respect to humanity. We learn early on to treat people like we want to be treated. Well, I want to be respected, and I want someone to speak with me in a kind manner. We shouldn't be ashamed to behave in a way that's caring. I want our employees to feel that they are treated with kindness, and I want to perpetuate the idea that it's okay around here to behave that way in this organization."*

The idea of performing acts of kindness is heartwarming to most of us. Consider, however, that we cancel out those acts of kindness when we are otherwise unkind in word or deed. Remember the adage *Sticks and stones may break my bones, but names will never hurt me?* If I asked you to remember unkind words that someone said to or about you during childhood, I'll bet you could come up with something quickly. It probably still stings a little (or a lot). Yet, head over to your favorite social media channel, and it won't take long for you to find examples of grown adults calling each other names and judging each other harshly. Turn on the television, and you'll see and hear leaders in powerful positions using derogatory language and insulting individuals and large groups of people. Somehow, this has become acceptable.

In the workplace, unkindness can manifest as gossip, hate-speech, blaming, shaming, incivility, and even bullying. You must cultivate a culture of kindness and compassion to create a positive and safe work environment. As "Kumbaya" as this may sound, numerous studies agree. According to *WalktheRidge.com*, "A poll of 800 managers and employees in seventeen different industries found that, among workers who had been on the receiving end of incivility:

- 48% intentionally decreased their work effort.
- 47% intentionally decreased time spent at work.
- 80% lost work time worrying about the incident.
- 66% said their performance declined.
- 78% said their commitment to the organization declined."[1]

The idea of focusing on kindness, compassion, and civility in the workplace isn't some idealistic vision of an unrealistic dreamer. It has a real-world, bottom-line impact on your organization. Ask Ron Green of Oregon Pacific Bank. In 2020, the company had been on an upward trend of improved financial conditions since the recession ten years prior, with a 35-percent increase in net operating income from 2018 to 2019. The culture of kindness has had its greater impact, Ron believes, in attracting new team members to the bank. *"People want to work in a place where there are smiles, and people doing things for each other, and where people say thank you and appreciate their coworkers."* When you have that kind of respect, it fosters engagement. Amid the 2020 pandemic, the bank received countless calls from small business owners—veterinarians, auto-mechanics, dentists, and others—on the verge of tears because they couldn't penetrate the infrastructure of their larger banks to get a Paycheck Protection Program (PPP) loan to keep their businesses afloat. Marketing manager Ellen Huntingdon said, *"It was so inspiring to see! Our employees had no second thought of what we were going to do to help them. We put in fourteen-hour days for weeks on end to make it happen for these small business owners. Not just our lending team, but everyone. Other departments picked up the slack here and there because we believe in the work we do, and we wanted to help our communities and businesses survive."*

So, yes, there are acts of kindness. However, you don't get that kind of commitment from your people unless they feel cared about and respected. According to Ellen, a passionate supporter of the culture at OPB, *"You work with the same people for forty hours plus a week, so you want to work in an environment where your voice can be heard, where you're respected, and where you treat each other with compassion."* Her coworkers agree. Oregon Pacific Bank was named by *Oregon Business Magazine* as one of the 100 Best Places to Work in Oregon for 2020 and 2021. Employee reviews proclaim, "The atmosphere makes it a joy to come to work every day," "friendly employees and even better customers," and "OBP is very supportive of their employees. It's the first place I've worked where there were so many long-term employees with ties to the community."[2]

If employee engagement and acts of generosity and compassion result from a culture of kindness, what is kindness if not a tangible act? I propose the following: curiosity, empathy, and respect. Let's take a deeper dive into these three critical skills, shall we?

CURIOSITY

I've never really been a huge sports fan. However, growing up in Westport, Massachusetts, there is one thing you know for sure: The Red Sox are good, and the Yankees are bad. Red Sox fans rock and Yankees fans, well, you know. Then I was hired as an actress in the Pennsylvania Renaissance Faire and lived in an old church with actors from all over the country. It was the first time I lived away from my New England home. One day I walked into the TV room to join my new friends. "The game" was on, and the Sox were playing another team. After a few minutes, this strange, unfamiliar sensation came over me when I realized that these new friends I loved so much were cheering for *(gasp)* the Yankees! Never in my life had I been in a room where people were rooting for anyone but the Red Sox. What was happening? Where the heck was I? Toto, I don't think we're in *Hah-ved Yahd* anymore.

Since my new friends were really, really cool, I rewrote my story about Yankees' fans. They can be pretty awesome people (apologies to my Sox-loving family and friends back home). As human beings, it's natural for us to "write stories" about other people and be a bit judgmental. The Red Sox example was light-hearted, but there have been other times in my life when I have rushed to judgment about the why and how of people's behavior. I've judged my husband, family, friends, and large groups of people who live lives different from the one I choose to live. We all do this. The key is to recognize that and stay open to new discoveries. Years ago, in 2015, my friend and colleague Jessica Pettitt spoke on the National Speakers' Association convention's main stage. It was a four-minute-and-thirty-seven-second presentation that had a lifelong impact on me. Here's what she said: *"We all write stories about other people. It's not 'don't write a story,' but it's 'recognize that you do.' What I implore you to do, and what I remind myself to do, is print that story as a draft, triple-spaced, with extra-wide margins. You do that because you're anticipating edits. When we do that, we're engaging with someone in a genuine, curious way. Genuine curiosity is seeking new information so that my story can become more accurate."*

While we may think we have everything and everybody all figured out, the truth is that none of us do. Our individual experiences shape our belief systems. When we get curious and, as Jess says, leave room for edits, we open the way to true kindness. Licensed clinical mental health counselor associate Christen Rinaldi agrees. Christen, who leads a counseling practice in Asheville, North Carolina, says, *"Instead of fostering a culture of kindness, consider fostering a culture of curiosity. Showing a genuine curiosity and interest in other people, without judgment (or at least putting judgment aside) leads to compassion and kindness."* She believes, and I agree, that every person hired for or promoted to a leadership position could benefit from an onboarding process that includes curiosity and compassion as part of their skills development.

When we employ curiosity at work, it means we stop ourselves from rushing to judgment and making decisions or pronouncements without getting all the facts. When I asked Ellen Huntingdon what they did at Oregon Pacific Bank when a team member's behavior was out of alignment with their value of respect, she said, *"Our staff is pretty conscious that perhaps this happened because someone is having trouble at home, or perhaps they're going through a hard time. The first level of action is to put the time into understanding what the issue is before any sort of corrective action is taken."* So often, we judge people when putting their behavior into context can help us gain a deeper perspective. Getting curious at work means:

• Admitting that you may not know everything there is to know.

- Becoming inquisitive and asking questions. The words *tell me more* can lead to magical discoveries when said with genuine interest.
- Listening first and being open to new ways of thinking.
- Being receptive to ways you can learn from people, even when you disagree with them, and refraining from gossip.
- Rejecting black and white thinking. Instead of thinking, *"This is good and that is bad"* or *"I'm right and he's wrong,"* remember that human reality is more nuanced, and there are more than fifty shades of gray.
- Allow yourself not to know. It's okay to wonder for a while.

As Jessica Pettitt reminds us, *"Leave room for edits."* Getting curious is the first step to deepening your perspective and seeing things from another's point of view. This brings us to the next skill to develop if you want to create a culture of kindness: empathy.

EMPATHY

You may remember Morgan Spurlock from his award-winning, famous documentary *Supersize Me,* in which he lived on McDonald's food for thirty days. He also produced a television documentary show that aired three seasons from 2005 to 2008. It was called *30 Days,* and the concept was to have people of different points of view or from different life experiences immerse themselves in the other one's life for thirty days. For instance, a Christian lived for thirty days with a person of the Muslim faith. A straight man lived with a gay man. A person who believed in gun owners' rights immersed themselves in the world of someone who believed in gun control, and vice versa. Spurlock himself volunteered to be locked in prison for thirty days to experience what that was like. In the end, while people didn't necessarily come out of their thirty-day experiment with entirely different views, their rhetoric was softer. In most instances, they were able to find common ground, get a sense of the other person's feelings, and emerged kinder and more empathetic human beings. At least, that was my experience as a viewer.

That show was all about empathy, which means to put yourself in the shoes of another human being and see, as best you can, from their perspective. To get a sense of what they must *feel* like. It's a life skill we could use more of in this day and age. It's a time in which not only does everyone have an opinion, but thanks to social media, we get to hear them all and engage in online arguments. The reality is that it's much more comfortable to think, *"I'm right, and they're wrong"* than to try to see a situation from another person's viewpoint. Yet, more empathy is exactly what's needed. Notice I don't say sympathy. Empathy and sympathy are very different. The traditional definitions are that empathy is feeling *with* someone, while sympathy is feeling *for* them. Empathy is the more difficult of the two because, as Dr. Brene Brown reminds us, to have empathy, you've got to allow yourself to be vulnerable. *"To connect with you, I have to connect with something in myself that knows that feeling,"* says Brown.[3] Often, that feels dangerous to do.

However, empathy doesn't mean we have to totally give up our belief systems. It does mean we can accept that others experience the world differently than we do, and we can find commonalities in terms of our human emotions. At Red-Carpet Learning, for instance, we teach employees how to show empathy when

dealing with an upset customer and have them practice seeing
the complaint or problem from the angry person's point of view.
They don't have to agree with the customer; they only have to
see things from their perspective. Leaders must also have empathy for their team members in these situations. Often, you
put your employees in circumstances where they are supposed to
deal with customer complaints and dissatisfied customers without ever being equipped to do so. Managers may be upset that
the employee didn't handle it correctly but put yourself in their
shoes, and you may realize they don't know how, and that's a
frightening place to be.

Leaders can also show empathy for their team members by:

- Considering their thoughts and feelings before making big
  decisions.
- Putting themselves in their team members' shoes by doing
  their jobs for a day or more.
- Listening more deeply and striving to see another person's
  perspective.
- Asking team members what they need to successfully do
  their jobs.
- Identifying their own biases and becoming open to the
  ideas of others.

Cultivating an empathetic workplace has become and will
continue to become increasingly important as workplaces become more diverse, and the priorities of your employees change.
According to the 2020 businessolver's® State of Workplace
Empathy Report, 76 percent of employees thought an empathetic organization inspires employee motivation and drives

greater productivity. Sixty-eight percent say their employer is empathetic, and 48 percent believe that organizations overall are empathetic.[4] These percentages were down from previous studies. Empathy has been consistently seen as important and tied to business impact by employees, CEOs, and HR professionals. Leaders who haven't been developing their aptitude for empathy will be behind the eight-ball. The good news is that most scientists today agree that most of us are born with the capacity for empathy and that it is a skill that can be taught and improved upon. Include empathy education and skills practice in your leadership development program if you want to cultivate a culture of kindness and respect.

RESPECT

Mike Domitrz founded The Center for Respect® after his sister was sexually assaulted in 1989, committing to do everything he could to prevent sexual violence from ever happening to others. At The Center for Respect, they work with corporations, schools, the government, military, and organizations of all kinds to help them build a more profound, stronger foundation of respect. As for the definition of respect, Mike says, *"When you ask people at all levels of an organization what it means to be respected, you hear the following: 'to be seen for exactly who I am and to always have a voice when I'm told I have a voice.'"*

Some feel that respect is reserved for people of authority or "important" people. However, if you accept the premise that every human being is important, respect boils down to the Golden Rule: Treat others as you would like to be treated. It's a principle that most of the world's great religions share:[5]

Christianity: *In everything, do to others what you would have them do to you. (Matthew 7:12)*

Judaism: *That which is hateful to you, do not to your fellow. That is the whole Torah; the rest is commentary. (Talmud, Shabbat 31a)*

Islam: *None of you believes until he wishes for his brother what he wishes for himself. (An-Nawawi's Forty Hadith 13)*

Buddhism: *Do not hurt others in ways you yourself would find hurtful. (Udanavarga 5:18)*

Hinduism: *This is the sum of duty: do nothing to others that would cause you pain if done to you. (Mahabharata 5:117)*

In essence, to be respectful is to treat each human being like they matter, and they deserve your consideration and courtesy. When you think of respect in those terms, you realize it's a necessity to creating a positive employee experience. Mike Domitrz agrees. *"Respect is not a standard of excellence. Respect is the bare minimum requirement."*

We all have moments of being respectful and disrespectful. Why? Because we're human, we've been hurt, and we have fears that cause us to be defensive. Some of that defensiveness manifests as disrespect. *"Bring up the idea of a disrespectful person, and we create this image of a monster in our head,"* says Mike. *"We know we're not monsters; hence the offenders must be other people, not us."* To that end, the team at The Center for Respect offers the 9 Daily Displays of Disrespect that almost everyone engages in:

1. Denying access. Mike explains, *"This can manifest as a male CEO going out to dinner with any of the male management or leadership but won't go alone with a female leader. He may feel*

it's to prevent harassment accusations, or his partner doesn't like it, but if you make those choices based on gender only, you're flat-out denying access. Or the group that sits together in the office and goes out to lunch every day, but Harry sits over here and never gets invited. Harry starts to feel devalued and like he's not part of the organization. This can happen racially, culturally, generationally, all kinds of things can play into it, but it's a form of denying access." This can also show up in the form of withholding information.

2. Dictator. "*The one who walks in and says, 'You're going to do this, and you're going to do it my way,' and now they think 'Well, I'm a strong leader.' However, there's a difference between leadership and dictatorship. If you're making all or most of your decisions and delegations without input, you might just be dictating instead of leading,*" says Mike.

3. Silence. "*For instance,*" says Mike, "*your partner or coworker throws out an idea to you that they're excited about. You just sit there. Now they feel like you're ignoring them. The truth may be that you are an analyzer. To keep from being disrespectful, a leader can say, 'Thank you for sharing. I'm very analytical. May I get back to you in two or three days so I can have time to process? I want you to know that I've heard you.'*"

4. Degrade. "*An example that often happens in the workplace is when you bring me an idea, and I respond with, 'Yeah, we've tried that before.' I don't even realize I just degraded you,*" says Mike. "*Your teammate has every right to wonder, 'Why didn't it work before? Maybe I can help you overcome that. You're not even giving me a chance. You're just degrading my idea right off the bat.'*" Another example is gossip which, according to Mike, can quickly result in someone being degraded.

5. Interrupt. *"High-energy passionate people will do this to fill pauses, and they think they're saving everyone time. One of my friends,"* says Mike, *"calls it 'efficient communication.' I ask him, 'What does your wife think about efficient communication?' He says, 'She hates it!' The moment your method or approach of communication does harm, it's no longer efficient.*

6. Bulldoze. *"The person in the meeting whose ideas will take up the whole hour,"* says Mike, *"They have no interest in hearing from you. They only care about sharing their own opinions."*

7. Fixer. *"People who think it's their job to fix other people."* Mike explains the most common version is when you read a book and think of all the people who could use the book's advice—when the only person that book is talking to at the time is *you.* Another great example Mike gives is jumping into other people's projects and offering solutions they didn't ask for. You know, "unsolicited advice"—fixing what others didn't ask you to fix.

8. Distracted. *"You're talking, and I'm multitasking,"* Mike shares. *"I look up at you off and on (or now and then I look at my phone while you are talking). Quickly you realize you are not my priority. You do not matter at that moment. Whatever I'm looking at appears to be more important. No one likes this feeling."*

9. Identity and Age Bias. *"This can manifest as denying access, but it can be its own creature. For instance, refusing to give credibility based on someone's age, or gender, or ethnicity, etc."*

Did you see yourself in any of these? Even if we don't *always* behave in these ways, most of us sometimes do. I have to admit, I see myself in number five and am constantly working on my disrespectful habit of interrupting. I would also add name-calling to the list of nine, which, perhaps, would fall under degradation. Somehow, in the advent of social media, this has become acceptable behavior. We laugh when celebrities on the Jimmy Kimmel show read mean tweets written by others about them. Are they funny, though? As much as we are wired to value and celebrate kindness, we seem to have discovered newfound freedom to ditch the golden rule and say anything, regardless of how it makes others feel.

Want a copy of the 9 Daily Displays of Disrespect from The Center for Respect? Go to www.CenterForRespect.com /EmployeesFirst.

To create a culture of kindness, you must make choices for respect. Understand that to respect does *not* mean:

- You have to agree with everyone.
- You put people up on a pedestal.
- You are obedient without question.

However, respect does mean that you make choices that are inclusive, caring, civil, uplifting, and transparent, and that provide equal opportunity.

———

Curiosity, empathy, and respect are all critical skills to develop if you want to cultivate an authentic culture of kindness. When your culture is rooted solidly in these three competencies, kindness and compassion are the results. Developing these three skills in your people, starting with leadership, is the foundation for preventing sexual harassment, discrimination, and bullying. It's deep and difficult work because it brings up our vulnerabilities, but otherwise, your organizational efforts amount to no more than a band-aid solution to major workplace problems. Mike Domitrz elaborates. *"Imagine a skyscraper and sexual harassment is on the 19th floor, and cultural diversity issues are on the 17th floor, and you've got bullying on the 23rd floor. Many companies focus solely on a specific floor. They incorrectly believe, 'If I just fix that floor, the rest of our company will be perfect.' Many organizational leaders don't realize that the foundation of the entire building is what's cracking, and that's why you're having all of those issues. Companies that come to us because they want to create a thriving culture of respect are going to succeed greater than those who only want to address the consequences of a lack of respect."* How do you cultivate a culture of kindness, curiosity, empathy, respect, and compassion? Start with the following actions.

DEVELOP YOUR LEADERS

Contrary to how many businesses often operate, it's not the frontline and back-of-the-house employees who must change first. It's management. To understand this, it's good to familiarize yourself with the idea of servant leadership (coined by Robert E. Greenleaf in an essay published in 1970 entitled "The Servant as Leader") and the inverted leadership pyramid. Traditionally, the chain of command looks like a pyramid, with the CEO at the top, followed by VPs, middle managers, supervisors, and then employees at the bottom. It had more to do with who got to tell who what to do, rather than any form of supporting each other. The decision-makers at the top and the do-ers at the bottom. Throughout the past couple of decades, there has been a slow adoption of an inverted pyramid, in which the CEO, the VPs, and middle management are at the bottom. Their sole job is to support the people at the top (employees) through mentoring, coaching, education, providing tools, and removing barriers so your frontline and back-of-the-house people can successfully serve your customers. In other words, the people in leadership positions are there to serve your employees. One way you do that is by role-modeling the culture you want to grow in your organization.

Often we think of a strong CEO as the one person who sets the tone for the organizational culture. However, if you continue in that vein alone, once the CEO leaves, the culture quickly disappears. Or there are sometimes "respect or kindness initiatives" that become the job of the human resources department instead of shared responsibility throughout the organization. Again, once that person leaves, there goes the "initiative." Says Ron Green, CEO of Oregon Pacific Bank, *"I'm the present figurehead today, but what we are doing in terms of our culture of kindness was here before me and will survive me long into the future."* This happens when you develop skills in all people in management positions, so the traits of curiosity, empathy, respect, kindness, and compassion are role-modeled by every leader in the organization. Then, kindness becomes part of your company's DNA and will naturally extend itself to your employees and customers.

To create a culture of kindness, invest in the education and give people a chance to develop their emotional intelligence skills, build their curious and empathetic muscles, and practice respectful language and leadership in a safe space.

HIRE AND PROMOTE ACCORDINGLY

Often, organizational leaders will spend days, weeks, or even months crafting their perfect core values and rolling them out in grandeur. However, when it comes to the people they hire, those values are secondary to a specific skill set. For instance, you make allowances for that person who speaks sharply or insults others but is one of your best salespeople. Or this person is a real bully, but boy, are they good with numbers. You purport to put people first, but you allow them to be belittled. In other words, your core values are a set of really great ideas, but you're only committed to them when it's convenient.

"Notice," says Mike Domritz, *"how few companies have the word* respect *in their core values. They'll say* integrity *or* customer service *or* caring for our customers, *but they don't say* respect. *However, when respect is the value, you don't have to say, 'We care about customers' or 'employees' or 'vendors,' because what you're saying is that you treat* all *human beings well."*

If you're ready to commit to leading a company or department where human beings are treated with respect and compassion, then those values must be front and center when you're hiring people. On the subject of hiring, Ron Green says, *"I want to have confidence that the person I'm hiring can build a relationship. For instance, we hired a CFO three years ago. She's got the education, the experience, and the technical side of the job down. Great! Before I hired her, I put that aside and did the best I could to glean if she could build and strengthen relationships with those she interacted with daily. Would she fit with our culture of kindness?"* Turns out the answer was yes, and she's been with the bank for the past three years. The point, however, is that if the answer to that second question was no or if Ron was unsure, he would keep looking because they are committed to this part of their culture.

Be relentless in looking for the people who have the strengths and values to bring your culture to life. You can use any number of assessments, for example, to determine someone's natural in-clinations. You can also use values-based questioning. Ask candi-dates to share an example of a time when they felt disrespected, or perhaps a time when they were disrespectful, and what they learned. Did they ever work in a situation in which they observed people being unkind to one another? What did they observe, and what would they do differently? Finally, include other members of the team in the interview process. Educate them so they be-come skilled interviewers and ask them to help determine which candidate is the best fit for your desired culture.

The same principles apply when you are promoting people in-ternally. Even today, leaders promote people because they excel at the task or getting financial results without much thought given to their relationship skills. If you go back to that concept of ser-vant leadership and the inverted pyramid, relationship-building should be the number-one skill you look for in a potential leader. Perhaps those skill-developing courses on curiosity, empathy, and respect could be prerequisites for anyone who wishes to move into a supervisory position at your company.

Finally, when you're ready to fully commit to a culture of kindness, *"You may also find there are some individuals in the organization, including leadership and management, who do not care and do not respect other human beings, and you have to let go of them,"* adds Mike Domitrz. *"You cannot say that respect is a value for your organization and then make an exception in which one person is allowed to be consistently disrespectful. If it's a real value, then disrespect and incivility aren't allowed to occur, and when they do, they are called out."*

Commitments like these are not easy. I know that I, along with my fellow consultants, wish that we had some magic fairy dust that you could sprinkle in your workplace to make every-one caring and kind, and work well together. A magic wand to make it easy to create an employee experience that promotes engagement, retention, and service excellence. The truth is that sometimes it's effortless, and other times it demands courage. Wouldn't you say it's worth it to have a team that feels valued?

GO UNDERCOVER

"To develop empathy for your employees," suggests Christen Rinaldi, LCMHCA, *"leaders can spend a week doing the tedious jobs in their organizations. Empty bedpans, work in the cafeteria, or check the badges at the front door. Often we get into a leadership role, and we forget the very ladder we climbed."*

Perhaps any team member whose job it is to support other team members could spend time working side-by-side with those employees and learning the ropes from their point of view. Years ago, I spoke for people who worked in the headquarters of a large senior living organization. These were the very people tasked with supporting those out in the senior living residences or "communities." I asked the group how many of them had visited one of their communities in the past twelve months. Out of a group of about seventy-five people, only ten or eleven raised their hands. What? How could these professionals make decisions that would affect the team (and consequently the elders they served) at the senior housing sites if they don't clearly understand what the day-to-day looks like? How could they be a "support office" without experiencing the core services the company delivered?

Want to increase your empathy quotient at work? It's time to go undercover.

For instance, at the Savannah Bananas, they've been engaging in a version of "Undercover Fan" for a while. One leader goes through the experience at each game, sometimes in disguise, as a fan in the stands. From parking to cheering, to concessions, and heading home, they experience what it's like to be a customer and report their experience back so they can make improvements. Recently, they added a new twist called "Frontline Fan." Leaders take turns working in a frontline role to get a sense of the experience from their teammates' point of view. They might be assigned the Parking Penguin job, take tickets, or work the beer garden. The idea is that they are experiencing what their employees are experiencing. *It was my night,"* recalls Jesse Cole, *"and the yellow tux is off, and my name tag says Toby. 'Toby, you're at the grills!' I head over there, and I've got a different hat on and a mask (because of Covid), but as soon as they hear my voice, my cover is blown. Regardless, I'm grilling with my team in the middle of the day, and I ask them to tell me more about the process. What can we do to make it better? I'm watching, and they are flipping 100 burgers on the grill and 100 burgers off the grill, and it's helping me develop real respect and empathy for what they do. They don't get any recognition. They're behind the scenes.*

'Okay, Toby! It's time to work the register,' they tell me. This is something I'd never done, so I get my training, and then it's show-time. From 5:30 pm to 8:45 pm, there wasn't a single break. Of course, they put me on register one. I had a runner with me named Patrick. He was a quieter member of our team, and I was told he was really good with tasks. So, after an hour, I get the hang of the register, and I start having fun! I'm juggling cookies and yelling 'C'mon down!' like the host of the Price Is Right. *'Are you ready for the best Coke of your life?' I ask my customers. Out of the blue,*

Patrick starts to get into it. I hear him shout, 'Best Coke of your life, coming right up!' and 'Here come the jalapeños!' We start yelling back and forth, and it's the most fun we've ever had."

Jesse reiterates, *"You've got to put yourself in the shoes of your people to have empathy. You can't just tell people to have purpose and pride. You need to see it, do it, feel it, emulate and develop empathy for what your people go through.* Toby got more tips than anyone that day, and he gave them all to Patrick.

Gaining empathy by walking in your team members' shoes was a recurring theme in the research for the 2020 What Makes an Employee Feel Valued Report. When asked for a final message she wanted to share with *Employees First!* and readers of this report, one respondent, who works in parks and recreation, said, *"I wish they were more aware of all that we do. We're not just doing programming for recreation. We do offer a zillion classes for our constituents, yes, but it's the million hidden things that you do that don't get logged but are the more meaningful aspects of your job. Often it's someone who calls you just because they're lonely, and they just want to talk, and you have to call them back after hours to check on them. Sometimes it's identifying someone who needs social services or noticing that someone's dementia is progressing. Those are the kinds of things you wish your supervisor understood. The hourly employee is typically the one on the frontline, and they have their pulse on what it means to serve. I often wish directors would spend an entire day—not just getting the phones for an hour while you're on break—but spend an entire day doing the job of one of your employees. Don't be a manager behind the wall or a desk in the administrative area. Come out in front because I think people need to be reminded of all the frontline people are facing every day."*

When was the last time you went undercover?

LISTEN DEEPLY

One of the best ways to show respect for your team members is to give them space to be heard and recognize the value of their voice and their experience. Listen without judgment and pre-conceived notions. It's not the first time we've talked about listening in this book, and it won't be the last, because it may be one of the most important things we can do to create a culture of kindness and a better employee experience.

Claude Silver is the chief heart officer of VaynerMedia, an advertising agency founded by entrepreneur, author, speaker, and internet personality Gary Vaynerchuk. She caught my attention when she was interviewed for Influence 2020, the (first time virtual) convention of the National Speakers' Association. When she finished speaking, I knew I wanted to be her best friend. I settled for a conversation. In that initial interview, Claude said that when discussing what she would do as chief heart officer, Gary told her, *"Your job is to touch every individual in this organization and infuse the company with empathy."* With close to 1,000 employees, that's no easy task, yet as Vaynerchuk's number two, she rises to the occasion. Claude takes building relationships very seriously, and whether it's across the table at lunch or through a screen on Zoom or Google Hangouts, she spends much of her time listening. *"I'm having fifteen-minute meetings with people and really listening to what's up with them, asking questions and probing a little, so I can understand how they're integrating into our culture, what they bring to our culture, what they need more or less of, and getting their ideas.* Claude elaborates, *"I'm very common sense about it. I don't have spreadsheets to tell me who to talk to, and I'm fortunate that I run on intuition. We're a high-touch organization, and when I say that I mean, we spend time with people. It's pretty simple and pretty mag-ical."* According to Claude, as of January 2020, employee reten-tion was at a high 85 percent. If Claude's job is to scale Gary, she also is developing culture champions to scale herself. *"Listening is an integral part of the culture. Gary's doing it, I'm doing it, and I've taught people on my team to do the same."*

They've got, as my friend Dave Timmons would say, a listen-ing strategy. What's your listening strategy? Your annual surveys aren't enough. Here are a few ideas:

- One-on-ones, in which you're talking less and listening more.
- Lunch with the boss. See above.
- Group discussions. Get team members in a room and ask them for their thoughts and opinions.
- Phone conversations. In my first book, *The Celebrity Experience* (Wiley, 2008), I wrote about Colin Reed, who was at the time the CEO of Gaylord Entertainment. He set up a day once a month when employees at any of the Gaylord properties could call and chat with him. They called to share ideas, complain, or praise someone, or sim-ply because they had never talked to the CEO before. It's how he stayed in touch with the heartbeat of the company.
- Start, stop, continue sessions. Gather your people together and give them index cards. Throw out a challenge or goal and ask your team what they think you (as a leader or the organi-zation) need to stop doing, start doing, and continue doing.

One word of advice: Don't listen if you're not going to act. One leader took my suggestion of hosting a start, stop, continue session. The next time I was at their site, she stopped me in the hall and told me how great it was. *"They even came up with an idea for a communication bulletin board!"* She was so excited. However, when I asked her where the bulletin board was, she sighed, *"Oh, I haven't had time to do it yet."* Her meeting had been two months earlier. Those team members were probably excited, too, until they realized their idea-sharing session was for naught. Not to mention that the leader in question could have delegated the job to her team, and they would have been glad to execute their own plan.

When asked what a culture of kindness meant to her, Claude Silver responded, *"Everything starts with being human. My purpose is to bring humanity into the workforce. To do that, we need to lean into what we all know to be true, which is we all feel a heck of a lot better when we are using those very human soft skills such as kindness, humility, compassion, empathy, gratitude, and warmth. For me, there is no culture without kindness and compassion. You might as well close your doors right now. Of course, I know many cultures exist without being rooted in kindness and emotional intelligence; however, those cultures won't be around for much longer. The world has changed, and you and I are in the middle of a transformation that has never happened in our lifetime. The move from the head to the heart is happening right now. We are moving to a world that values heart and empathetic leadership and values someone caring about them and wanting them to grow and develop as much as you want yourself to grow and evolve. We're moving into the collective 'we' and not the 'I,' and leaders better get on board if they want to be here for the long haul."*

Start by listening deeply.

DEVELOP A STYLE GUIDE

"This is one of the kindest places I've ever worked at," Hailley Griffis, head of public relations for Buffer, told me. *"Even as a mostly remote workplace, there are no passive-aggressive messages or big angry question marks or emojis. Everyone defaults to being nice, and if we aren't clear about something, we just ask questions."* When asked why she thought this was, Hailley told me about learning the Buffer language and the "way we talk to each other" when she first joined the company. *"It starts with how we speak to our customers. When a customer calls in with a tech issue, we never say, 'Well, it's because you did this or that.' Instead, we ask, 'Would you be up for trying a couple of things to see what works?' We speak respectfully to our customers, and it translates into how we talk to each other."*

After our conversation, I did a little digging and found the Buffer Style Guide. If you're in marketing or graphic design, you might think this is a document that spells out the fonts, colors, and style of your online and in-print presence. Instead, the company-wide Buffer Style Guide offers guidance for team members on how to act and speak the language of the Buffer Way.

The style guide talks about Buffer's tone being relatable, genuine, inclusive, and informed by empathy. *Buffer,* it reads, *would be the kind of person you want to grab a cup of coffee with.* It dives deep into diversity and inclusion, what words and phrases to use, and what not to use. It goes into how to invite people rather than command them and that the words *I'm sorry* are also appropriate.

You might even go a little deeper regarding respectful language at your company. What does it look like, and what does it sound like? Here's an example: *"We refrain from staring at our phones at our company as we walk down the hallway. Instead, we proactively look people in the eyes, smile, and provide a friendly greeting."*

Consider what your culture of kindness guide could look like, create it and then make it part of your onboarding curriculum.

INVEST IN YOUR OWN PERSONAL DEVELOPMENT

As a leader in your company, one of the greatest gifts you can give yourself and the people you lead is to dive deep into your personal psychology. As much as we may try to leave our humanity at the door when we head to work, the truth of the matter is that it's impossible. We're all human. We have all built up protections from the myriad hurts and slights we may have experienced in our lifetimes. We all have our triggers. Those words and actions cause us to put up those protective barriers and lash out at other people with judgment, or defensiveness, or a lack of empathy and compassion. To be the best leader you can be, bravely go where you've never gone before. This may mean investing in emotional intelligence education, becoming aware of what causes you to have a lapse in respectful behavior or good old-fashioned therapy. The more self-aware you become, the better leader you'll be, and the more your team members will feel seen, heard, and respected.

EXPECT MORE

None of us are perfect, nor will we ever be. However, we can expect more of ourselves and each other. Most people would probably consider me a kind person. Yet, I have my moments. If you caught me glaring at people who weren't wearing masks at the grocery store during the 2020 pandemic, you might have considered me an angry person. You may have seen a Facebook post or two written in frustration that was less than loving. Yes, I've even had my pet "names" for a neighbor or two. However, I want to expect better of myself, and I invite you to do the same. If you considered your social media page and comments part of your legacy, would you be proud of them? Do they reflect the kind-hearted person you are? Do they reflect the world you want to live in? The workplace culture you want? Yes, it's human to gossip and call each other names and get defensive and judgmental—but it's also human to be kind, loving, empathetic, and respectful. In every interaction, we get to make a choice, and the more intentional we are with those choices, the closer we are to kindness.

BACK TO THE BANK

When his boss came into his office to ask if he had heard about the fire that had started in Ashland, Thomas Russell, Operations Lead at Oregon Pacific Bank, wasn't concerned. He lived in the nearby town of Talent, but he trusted the fire department would act on it quickly. *"Yes, we have fires in the west, but you always expect it to be elsewhere, not your own home."* However, a few hours later, after conversations with a few evacuating neighbors, he realized the situation was serious. He stayed with a friend in Grants Pass for a couple of weeks and soon learned that his entire neighborhood, including the house he was renting, had completely burned down. *"It was extremely emotionally taxing,"*

Thomas confides, *"especially for an extravert like me who was already struggling with having to be on lockdown."* He lost everything he owned, including the video of his parents' wedding, which he was transferring to DVD as a gift for them. His coworkers at Oregon Pacific Bank immediately jumped in to help. One person took him shopping to get work clothes. Others texted him when they were out and about to see if he needed anything. Coworkers brought him food, clothing, and essentials to help him get through. It's this kind of caring that happens when you cultivate empathy, curiosity, respect, and kindness at work. Exclaims Thomas, who is happily settling into his new home, *"It just really shows the selflessness of the people we have here at Oregon Pacific Bank."* He adds, *"It's just a chapter in the book of my life, and hopefully, I can use it to support someone else in the future."*

Imagine a world where the number-one thought is *How can we support each other?*

CHAPTER FOUR

Roll Out the Red Carpet on Day One!

It's your first day at work for Talent Plus! It's a consulting firm that uses talent-based assessments and a scientific process to help companies worldwide select and develop candidates with the best talent and potential for excellence. You've been through a rigorous selection process, and you're excited to get started.

You'll start your first day with a few other colleagues who were also hired in the past month. At Talent Plus, all new hires begin on a single day each month, a day deemed their "Great Take Off Day!" Says EVP, communities, Cydney Koukol, *You only have one first day, and we want it to be memorable. Our leadership and colleagues invest a lot of time to make that day count, so doing that once a month is cost and time-effective.*"

If your first day starts within the walls of their beautiful offices in Lincoln, Nebraska, you and your other newly hired colleagues will be treated to a red-carpet welcome. Your new colleagues roll out a long red carpet in their bright and sunny atrium and line up on either side, providing an enthusiastic and warm welcome as you enter. You may notice your name beaming out from an electronic sign. If you're working from home, you'll be surprised and delighted by the beautiful "swag bag" that arrives on your doorstep.

You'll join your new colleagues and be introduced at Formation, a daily fifteen-minute practice when the entire Talent Plus team gathers (in-person or virtually) to review one of their core values, give recognition shout outs or "Plays of the Day" to coworkers or clients, celebrate birthdays and anniversaries, and make any necessary announcements.

Then there's "Focus on You." Talent Plus's senior leaders meet with you for about ninety minutes for the sheer purpose of getting to know you better. During this time, they frame the meeting so you (the new colleague) and the senior leaders may ask any questions, personal and professional. Megan Leasher, chief solutions strategist, a new addition to Talent Plus, shared, *"What stood out to me is that everyone at Talent Plus focuses on wanting to get to know each other at a deeper level, and this starts on day one. It built an immediate, powerful, intentional connection with each colleague I met."* Kyle Bruss, director of talent acquisition, adds, *"Starting at a new company can be nerve-wracking, so getting to know the executive leadership team on day one for an extended period may seem like an expensive investment. Still, when you say relationships are important, you have to live that value. Talent Plus does that in spades, and it's an investment in time and relationship building that pays dividends in creating a great company culture."*

The rest of your first day, and week, are spent getting to know the Talent Plus culture through a series of experiences, led by leaders and teammates, called the Colleague Learning Academy. At day's end, you and your fellow new hires will be the guests of honor at the "Great Take Off Day" celebration. You may invite your spouse, children, and other family members to attend as well. At the in-person version, there will be cocktails and hors d'oeuvres. During the virtual version, Talent Plus plays a "get to know your new colleague" trivia game using video conference technology to bring the company together in meeting you.

During this end-of-day celebration, attended by all Talent Plus colleagues and your guests, you will receive your Talent Card. Dr. Megan Leasher shares, *"The Talent Card presentation is the culmination of the event! It is a personalized, motivating summary of your assessment results, all of the great things we learned about you, and the reasons we selected you to join the Talent Plus family. Not only are the assessments accurate, but the Talent Card 'hits home' in a way that pulls your 'heartstrings and wows your friends and family in attendance.'"* It's an individualized, framed certificate that has three sections:

1. We like you because. . . .
2. You have these strengths. . . .
3. Here's what we expect of you. . . .

All of the Talent Plus founders sign the card, and, like many of your new colleagues, you will probably proudly display it on your desk.

During your second and third weeks, you'll spend time learning to conduct and analyze a Talent Plus in-person interview. Since this company you now work for is in the business of using science to help their clients select the absolute best talent, it's vital that everyone at Talent Plus, regardless of your title, can interview candidates for one of your customers.

Of course, they don't roll up the red carpet once your three weeks are up. The team at Talent Plus has a variety of best practices for showing appreciation for colleagues. Former president and current Talent Plus fellow Larry Sternberg was not above writing a thank-you letter to your mom if you did something above and beyond. The appreciation, however, starts on day one.

The new hire experience is a constant evolution at the company. When Dr. Megan Leasher, chief solutions strategist, was hired, she scheduled a virtual cup of coffee with every member of the Talent Plus team. She now suggests that all new colleagues are proactive in terms of getting to know their coworkers. As time goes on, and we have a better understanding of the future workplace, I expect the experience will undergo several evolutions.

There is one thing that the Talent Plus leadership team understands: A colleague's first day is a critical opportunity to build a meaningful relationship and one that most organizations squander on paperwork and compliance. In a virtual world, it's gotten even worse. Cydney Koukol shares, *"I have two nieces who graduated from college in May (2020) and have started new jobs, and neither have ever been inside their offices or met any of their colleagues in person. It's a very different world."*

True. It is a very different world. Yet, some things remain the same, and the way you onboard a new employee during their first few weeks sets the stage for how well they integrate into your company culture. Many studies connect the employee onboarding experience with how likely a new hire will stay with your company for several years.

When I speak to audiences about their new hire's first day, I ask them, *"How do you want your team member to feel during their orientation and onboarding?"* The answers come easily: *Inspired. Excited. Welcome. Prepared. Energized. Eager. In love with our company!* The follow-up question is: *"Does your current first-day experience or onboarding process consistently generate those feelings?"* A murmur of *"not so much"* ripples through the crowd.

The problem is that most first days are filled with compliance-driven activities. The paperwork to be filled out, the education that fulfills requirements, and the policies that must be discussed. Are you yawning yet?

In preparing to write this chapter, I crowd-sourced my social media buddies and asked, *"Has anyone had a really great first day on the job?"* One of the respondents replied, *"I've had a lot of jobs in my life, and I can't think of one! Most of the time, people were not prepared for you because they seemed very busy/overwhelmed."* Often, those in management positions are busy putting out fires or looking for quick fixes to problems such as employee turnover and disengagement because they didn't take time to properly welcome new hires in the first place.

It's time to reimagine the new hire experience and roll out the red carpet for incoming teammates. Start by listening to your current team. Ask, *"On a scale of 1 to 5, where 1 is 'not at all,' and 5 is '100%,' how welcome, prepared, and in love with our company did you feel during your first few days on the job?"* Then, ask the second question: *"If you gave us anything less than a 5, what could we have specifically done to make that a 5? Or, if you did give us a 5, what did we specifically do that made it a 5?"*

This chapter could end right here. If you haven't guessed by now, I'm a firm believer in asking the people closest to the dilemma how to solve it. Everyone who has worked for you has had a first day and some kind of onboarding. Ask them what worked and what didn't, act on their suggestions, and—*shazam!*—a better experience.

Having said that, sometimes people don't know what they don't know, so let me share a few additional ideas. Your employees may be so used to the typical rushed "welcome," full of policies, procedures, and paperwork, that they don't realize it could be so much more.

A red-carpet welcome involves three different steps and four elements. The three steps are the employee's first day, orientation, and onboarding. Onboarding is the long-term process of fully integrating your new team member into your company and culture, and providing the tools and education they need to be productive and do their job well. Orientation is a one-time event. It can be one or two days, one or two weeks, or even an entire month, but it's a one-time event at the beginning of an employee's tenure. Its purpose is to introduce people to their new workplace. The first day is . . . well, the employee's first day on the job. They might be starting at your location, from their home office, or anywhere in the world, but it's the day they first report for work. An employee's first day and the orientation event are part of the overall onboarding process, and there are four essential elements to include.[1]

Culture: Capture your team members' hearts right out of the gate by introducing them to your culture and helping them fall in love with your company.

Connection: Help your new people network and make friends by creating intentional coworker and leadership connection opportunities.

Communication: Deliver a red-carpet experience by communicating consistently and creatively with candidates and hiring manager/leadership teams. (Also known as Clarification.)

Compliance: The policies, the procedures, the paperwork, and all the required preparation needed so your new team member can legally and effectively start their job. You know this part well. Most onboarding experiences begin and end with compliance. We'll focus the rest of this chapter on the other three elements.

CULTURE

It's clear that you get an immediate sneak peek into their culture on your first day at Talent Plus. The red-carpet welcome, attendance at Formation, the Great Take Off Day celebration, and your Talent Card presentation are an immediate immersion into the company's culture.

Assuming you've hired well and you have a purposeful company culture, this is the part that produces the feeling of excitement within your new colleagues. It's the part that makes them glad you chose them, and they chose you. It's also the part that assures they assimilate into your culture and add positively to it, rather than letting their experiences in past organizations impact it negatively. Some establishments take their culture so seriously they have dedicated a significant portion of the onboarding experience to just that.

If you read my first book, *The Celebrity Experience: Insider Secrets to Delivering Red Carpet Customer Service* (Wiley, 2008), you were introduced to High Point University (HPU), a private educational institution located in North Carolina. They bill themselves at The Premier Life Skills University, and their brand promise is that every student receives an extraordinary education in an inspiring environment with caring people. Since 2005, under the leadership of University President Dr. Nido Qubein, they have grown exponentially in acreage, academic schools, and enrollment and won numerous awards. Every staff and faculty member at HPU attend a half-day course they call Culture Orientation as part of their onboarding process. The class, which has been conducted since 2007, is led by Gwenn Noell, assistant vice president for family services. The mandatory course for all new hires is meant to provide employees with an excellent basis for a successful tenure. The class introduces attendees to the history of HPU and, says Gwenn, *"who we were, who we've become, and the journey we took to get here."* Gwenn is also a parent of two HPU students, so she has a relevant perspective on the impact of HPU culture.

All top academic programs are reviewed, giving each new staff member a broader view beyond their center of focus. Dr. Nido Qubein inspires attendees with his personal story of immigrating to the United States from the Middle East. An HPU graduate himself, Nido has since become extremely successful as an entrepreneur, speaker, author, and serving on many boards including BB&T, the La-Z-Boy Corporation, and Great Harvest Bread Company, in addition to becoming president of the University. Employees learn how HPU gives back to the community and the economic impact the university has had on its surrounding area. They share stories of team members living the brand promise, such as the security guard whose job it is to keep the campus safe but greets each visitor with a big smile and an enthusiastic welcome. They share behind-the-scenes information about the process behind the promise, learning the importance of removing friction points, walking in the students' shoes, and choosing the customer over their own convenience. There is a university tour, and they spend a great deal of time talking about the HPU promise. Gwenn points out, *"It's important to arm your staff with the way to talk about your organization."*

What can you do to intentionally immerse new coworkers in your culture? Share stories that bring your culture to life, involve them in company traditions, invite your customers to give presentations, and get them talking to each other about your core values. Your culture is where your new hires will be living for the duration of their employment. It deserves a proper introduction.

CONNECTION

"When a new full-time teammate joins the Savannah Bananas team," reports Fans First director Marie Matzinger, *"their first two weeks are completely mapped out for them, down to the hour. Everyone they will be with and everything they'll be doing. We don't want people to come in not knowing who to talk to, or who to eat lunch with, or all those little nuances of getting used to a new environment."* Part of that onboarding process is making sure the new teammate meets as many of their coworkers as possible. In fact, it's part of the selection process. *"They meet and spend time with everyone they're going to be working with, and we don't officially hire them until the end of that first day, and we get the thumbs up from everyone on the team."* Over the first two weeks, they are learning some skills, learning about the Bananas culture (through the Fans First 101 Course), and spending time with several of their coworkers along the way.

If you've ever shown up on the first day of a new job and been thrown in, trial by fire, and not given a chance to connect with and learn from new coworkers, you know it's not the kindest way to treat a person. Gallup research has repeatedly shown that employees are more likely to be engaged and productive when they have a best friend at work.[2] Give people a head start by consciously connecting them with coworkers from the get-go.

When Claude Silver, chief heart officer at Vaynermedia, checks in on new hires, she often tells them, *"Hey, I'm going to introduce you to ten people (within the organization) that are phenomenal."* She then facilitates ten coffee conversations between coworkers, who are happy to connect. *"Imagine how it feels if I'm writing to you and saying, 'Hey, would you spend time with this person?' It means I trust you and our colleagues want to do right by our culture."* Connecting coworkers in this way is how the culture spreads, assuming you're linking them with teammates that embody your values.

There are numerous ways to build connection. Include icebreakers into your orientation, intentionally provide people with lunch partners, and involve current team members in the red-carpet welcome. Host coworker events (in-person or virtual) at which people can mingle and get to know each other. You can even begin before they're hired by having team members send welcome notes to new hires before their first day, inviting them to lunch or coffee, or for a video chat.

Remember also to allow plenty of time for your new hires to spend with their direct supervisor. A 2017 report by LinkedIn Talent Solutions called "Inside the Mind of Today's Candidate" surveyed more than 14,000 global professionals about their job-seeking attitudes and habits. Here's what respondents said in terms of what was most important to them during the employee onboarding process:

- 72% said that one-on-one time with their direct manager was most important.
- 67% wanted an outline of performance goals.
- 57% thought a plan for the first few weeks on the job would be helpful.

- 53% rated an introduction to the company culture and values as critical.
- 52% would appreciate a list of people to meet.[3]

As you can see, time with you—their direct manager—was number one on the list. It's something you can't afford to skip.

COMMUNICATION

In my experience working with Red-Carpet customers on their onboarding process, most of the frustration new hires feel is from a lack of clear communication. Sometimes it's communication overload! Are you sending your new team members so much detailed information that you're putting them to sleep?

Other sources of exasperation are a lack of clarification in terms of what's expected and poor coordination between hiring managers and departmental leadership. To provide the best experience for your new employees, clean up your communication practices.

Start by eliminating the siloed approach and get the entire onboarding team working together to improve the experience. By this, I mean human resources, hiring managers, departmental supervisors, mentors, and anyone involved in welcoming new employees. Choose a central location for sharing information. Assign tasks to the appropriate owners and designate one person to oversee the entire experience, checking in to ensure each person does what's necessary.

A best practice is to meet monthly and do what the Red-Carpet team calls a Take Two™. Review recent onboarding efforts and decide what we did well, what we could have done better, and what we'll do next time to improve.

Look at every bit of communication you send to new hires and ask, *"Is this red carpet or red tape?"* Eliminate every piece of paper or email that isn't necessary and give what's left a face-lift by making it more visually appealing, using videos, or sending reminder texts. You might even create an app where new hires can review checklists and get reminders.

Speaking of checklists, be sure to provide your new teammates with an itinerary of their own. Encourage them to take some responsibility for their own onboarding by keeping track of each step and checking them off when completed.

Finally, check back in regularly. Nothing says "We don't care" like setting a new person loose and then never talking to them again. Celebrate them every step of the way.

MAKE IT MEMORABLE

"It was two years ago, but I remember it like it was yesterday," gushes Christy Van Der Westhuizen, VP of sales and marketing for MBK Senior Living. *"It was my first day and I was greeted by a big sign with my name on it. The friendly concierge was waiting for me to walk me back to my new office, and lots of smiling faces waved at me along the way. The office was filled with swag. A jacket, a hat, pens, notepaper, flowers and plants. My name tag and business cards were front and center. I felt expected and that everyone was excited to have me join the team. Lunch was a get-to-know-you session and I was right at home."* The MBK team replicates that kind of reception for every new person who joins the home office. Consider the big to-do you have when a beloved coworker is retiring or leaving for another opportunity. What if you put that same effort into making new people at *all*

levels of the organization feel expected, welcome, and as if you're excited to have them?

Ever wonder what it takes to get an hourly employee who has never received red-carpet customer service to give it? You must give it to them, and it starts on day one.

CHAPTER FIVE

Start Spreading the News

Imagine what it would feel like if everyone on your team knew everyone else's exact salaries. Did that sentence frighten you a bit? If you worked at Buffer.com, it would be par for the course. Founded in 2010 by CEO Joel Gascoigne and Leo Widrich, Buffer is a technology company that allows you to schedule, publish, and analyze your social media posts. *"Like many similar companies,"* says Hailley Griffis, head of public relations, *"Buffer started as a side project, and when Joel launched it, he was sharing a lot about his journey."* True. In early 2011 Joel was sharing the number of signups and other company milestones with his social media audience. *"Our commitment to transparency is really about trying to help people. The information we share can help other entrepreneurs that are just starting out."* As the company has grown from a startup with four users to 73,000 customers and eighty-five teammates in nineteen countries, its commitment to transparent communication has been front and center. Default to transparency is their number-one core value, and the beliefs that power the principle are:

- As individuals, we view transparency as a lifestyle of authenticity and honesty.

- As a team, we view transparency as an effective way to work remotely and establish a culture of trust.
- As a company, we view transparency as a tool to help others.
- We share early in the decision process to avoid "big revelations."
- We strive to make all communication clear and avoid making assumptions.[1]

Visit the Buffer.com About page, and you'll see they take this commitment to transparent communication seriously. You can view up-to-date details about the level of diversity in their organization, plans for the future of their product, cultural successes and failures via their open blog, and, yes, their salaries. Originally they opened up the salary amounts to internal team members only, and later they made them public on their website.

When it comes to open communication, the leaders at *Buffer.com* believe in sharing the good, the bad, and the ugly. *"For instance,"* says Hailley, *"our diversity and inclusion numbers are not necessarily flattering. We definitely skew younger and white, so this is a good example of being transparent even if we're not at our best. We used to have many more male employees than female. Now we're at about 50/50. Putting our numbers on the website, and blogging about our diversity journey, holds us accountable for making positive changes. The reality is that many companies aren't in a great place when it comes to diversity, and often people don't want to share that information until they're in a good place. However, I think it takes away from the journey. Now we can share 'here's where we were, here's where we are, and here's where we're going.'"*

Being transparent about the hard stuff has other benefits as well. In 2016 the company went through a cash flow crisis that caused them to lay off some team members. Says Hailley, *"It was tough for Joel* [the CEO], *and obviously the people who were no longer with the company. Most companies try to hide when they've had layoffs because it doesn't always reflect well, but we shared that it had happened, why it happened, and what we were going to do to change. We hoped that it would help other companies going through the same thing, but also, job offers started to pour in for the people who were let go. It was a beautiful full circle."*

Of course, they also celebrate the good, including the financial stability Buffer.com achieved in later years, giving them the ability to buy out their investors to the tune of $3.3 million and successfully, although not easily, ride out the pandemic in 2020.

While this level of transparency may not be comfortable for many organizations, there is no doubt that a higher level of open communication is imperative if you wish to improve the employee experience. One of my projects in 2020 was to reach out to my customers and the Red-Carpet Learning community and just listen to what they were going through and their thoughts about how they would move forward. On one of those calls, the CEO of a nonprofit company told me that what surprised him most was how much his customers and employees appreciated his regular communications. He provided weekly email updates about what was happening related to the virus, and their organization and the recipients were vocal about their gratitude. It may have surprised him, but it didn't surprise me. There's no doubt that organizational leaders stepped up their communications during the COVID-19 pandemic to a level that would have been beneficial pre-pandemic. Low morale, mistrust, gossip, negativity, absenteeism, and turnover can, more often than not, be traced back to little or no communication.

On the other hand, companies like Buffer.com, whose leaders focus heavily on internal (and, frankly, external) communication, are reaping the rewards. In August 2018, Buffer's employee retention rate was 94 percent, and when asked, *"How long do you plan to stay at Buffer?"* Fifty-nine percent of respondents said they want to stay as long as possible, and 21 percent said they planned on staying five or more years. Consider that the average tenure for tech companies is 1.76 years. The field of technology has an employee turnover rate of 13.2 percent, whereas Buffer.com had 5.8 percent as of 2018.[2]

As with any organization, many factors contribute to employee retention. This book addresses most if not all of them. However, you can bet that Buffer's default to transparency and commitment to communication is one of the secrets to their success.

One of the other benefits to Buffer's extreme transparency is attracting the right people for their culture. *"When we made our salaries public,"* says Hailley, *"the number of applications sky-rocketed. As a company, one of the most challenging things in terms of hiring is finding qualified people who are aligned with your values. Making our pay and pay formula transparent resulted in double the number of applications because people knew they'd be paid fairly."*

Internal communications are also of the utmost importance when you have a remote or hybrid workforce. Says Hailley, *"We've been fully remote for a very long time now and in nineteen different countries. The commitment to transparency means there are no secrets. We don't think 'I can't share with that team because I have to keep it within my own team.' Everything is shared, which works because your manager might be asleep in another time zone when you need certain information."*

Honor your team members by giving them consistent and transparent information. However, know that providing information is only one of the three critical types of communication that impact the employee experience. They are informational, interpersonal, and inspirational. We'll take a deeper dive into all of them. In the meantime, here's another important "I word" when it comes to workplace communication: intentional.

WHAT'S MY MOTIVATION?

If you're someone who goes to the theatre, you may think it's impressive that the actors can "remember all those lines." Actually, the real work is determining *why* the character is saying the line at all—their motivation or intention. Says Angie Flynn-McIver, *"An actor doesn't talk on stage unless they are trying to make something happen. In life, however, unlike in the theatre, a lot of our communication can come from a default place where we forget there will be an impact that results from that thing we say."* Angie is the president of Ignite CSP (Coaching, Speaking, Presenting), and the co-founder of North Carolina Stage Company in Asheville and director of one of my all-time favorite theatrical productions, *Angels in America* at NC Stage. As president of Ignite CSP, she and her team help people create connection with other people more intentionally and deliberately. The same principles apply whether you're talking with someone one-on-one, leading a small meeting, or giving a keynote to 5,000 people. Says Angie, *"Intention is the engine behind all our communication. We want to make something happen, whether to get someone to pass the salt or save the whales. The stakes can be tiny or huge, but we always want something to shift and change. We can be deliberate about that outcome and thoughtful about our communication, or we can just say whatever comes to mind and let the chips fall where they may.*" A leader who cares about the people they lead will become more mindful about what they say and how they say it. It's where emotional intelligence and practicing self-regulation come to play. It means becoming more self-aware, knowing your default communication style, and being able to adjust it depending on the person(s) you're speaking with and the situation. *"We would have fewer issues with communication if we got radically candid with ourselves about where we're coming from most of the time,"* concludes Angie.

Ever say, *"Sticks and stones may break my bones, but words will never hurt me?"* Turns out we were wrong. Words matter. When you speak, the words you say have an impact and an outcome. People have used words to excite and incite. To stir people into action or suppress them. To make others feel good or bad. To build bridges or walls. To declare love or war. When leaders are reckless with their words, there are sometimes difficult, even harmful, and devastating consequences.

It's imperative that, as leaders, we are more thoughtful with our communications. Even the way you structure a sentence can have an impact. For instance, a study done in 2018 on expressions of gender equality by Eleanor Chestnut and Ellen Markman showed that even a simple sentence like *"Girls are as good as boys at math"* has the probable unintended consequences of implying that boys have more raw talent when it comes to math than girls do. A simple change to *"Girls and boys are equally good at math"* has a whole new meaning.[3]

Of course, you don't necessarily have the time to think through every word that comes out of your mouth. However, when the stakes are high, such as when you're having one-on-ones with employees or addressing the team as a group, it's important to know thyself and spend a little more time preparing for the impact you want to have and the message you want to send. When it comes to communication, intention is everything. This brings us to the three types of internal communication.

Informational: Freely and consistently sharing knowledge with other members of your team.

Interpersonal: How you verbally and non-verbally share that information with others.

Inspirational: Communicating on an emotional or "heart" level to move others to action.

INFORMATIONAL COMMUNICATION

You're stuck in the middle of the tarmac, on a plane going nowhere. There are two types of pilots. There's the silent one who leaves you wondering what's happening. They may give you an initial briefing, but afterward, you sit there counting the minutes and making up scenarios in your head as to the problem. *Is it the weather? Terrorists? What's wrong with the plane? There is no phalange!* (That was for my fellow *Friends* fans.) The other pilot gives you an initial explanation and provides you with updates every five or ten minutes, even if he's unsure of the ultimate time of takeoff. Which do you prefer? If you're like me, it's the second pilot. You'd rather know what's going on, even if it's terrible news, than sit there and wonder. It's the same for your team. When you don't let them know what's happening, the grapevine forms, and the rumors circulate. Then, it's on to damage control. Better to be up-front and provide consistent and honest updates.

Gallup research shows that how leaders communicate with their employees is the top internal communication factor related to employee engagement.[4] Another Gallup study found that 74 percent of employees feel they are missing out on company news.[5] At the very least, your team deserves to easily get their hands on the information they need to do their job effectively. Often, the breakdown happens between mid-level managers and supervisors and their direct reports, the frontline and back-of-the-house staff.

Several years ago, I was working with an organization that gave tours to their prospective customers. The executive director and mid-management level leaders met daily and received information about who was touring the building and when. The communication ended there. We made two simple changes. The first change was that managers would now share that information with their direct reports in morning stand-up meetings. The second change was that we educated the employees on their crucial role during these tours and how to make prospective customers feel welcome. The result was an increase in sales and a shorter sales cycle. Booyah!

It's true that in a world where many people will be working from home, in addition to those who work at your location, that transparent sharing of information with your team members at all levels will be of utmost importance. However, it always has been. Without the sharing of information, everything stops. Yet so many organizations have departments who work in silos, forgetting or refusing to share information with each other. Another barrier to transparent communication comes when you have people (usually senior leaders and mid-level managers) who are the gatekeepers of all information. Employees must ask for details rather than have them readily available. Ideally, your communication channels run throughout the organization:

Upward communication: Employees provide information and feedback to leaders.

Downward communication: Leaders provide information and feedback to employees.

Sideways communication: Coworkers and departments share information.

Here are some ways you can improve internal informational communication.

COME OUT FROM YOUR OPEN-DOOR POLICY

You might be thinking, *"Wait just a minute, Donna! Didn't you just say transparency is important? What's wrong with an open-door policy?"* What's wrong is that it's passive, not active. You can tell your team, *"My door's always open!"* but many, many people will never walk through that door. They have ideas and questions and concerns, but the nature of your position as a "boss" provides an invisible line that many people are too uncomfortable to cross. So, they save those thoughts and concerns for the grapevine or your one-time-a-year employee survey, or they never share them at all. It's time to come out from behind your desk. Intentionally walk around the building and engage people in conversations. Ask them questions. Catch them doing their best work. Get to know them as individuals. Set appointments for one-on-one meetings with employees. Form quarterly focus groups made up of diverse employees at every level of the organization and invite new people each quarter. Host weekly "lunch with the boss" sessions. For instance, Nido Qubein, president of High Point University, makes it a habit to walk around the university and meet students, prospective students, and parents. He attends games and theatrical performances, and personally hands out holiday candy. When I asked him, *"How do you have time to do all of that? You're such a busy man!"* he replied, *"I don't have time not to do it. The relationships I build by being out among our students, faculty, and staff is one of the secrets to our success."* If you have a virtual team, proactively reach out via your video-conferencing platform. Come out from behind your open door and build relationships with your people.

USE MULTIPLE CHANNELS AND GET CREATIVE

To get your message out to the masses, it's essential to understand that we all get our information from different sources and absorb it in our own way. For instance, you may have managers and supervisors who are on your intranet or have company email. However, if the only way you communicate is through online sources, you'll leave behind your team members who don't have computers or company email addresses. Additionally, according to a survey by Prescient Digital Media, only 13 percent of employees use their company intranet daily, and 31 percent admitted they had never used it![6] Also, what about the people on the second or third shift? Do they have the same access to information that the people on the first shift do?

Get intentional about the channels you use as you start spreading the news.

There are numerous options in terms of digital tools now—and will undoubtedly be even more by the time you're reading this book. As an organization whose team spans nineteen time zones, Buffer uses a combination of synchronous (in real-time) and asynchronous (at different times) tools to keep communication flowing between employees. They include Zoom, Slack (one of my favorites), Google Calendar, Dropbox, Threads, and Notion. Various online project management tools, such as Asana or Monday.com, allow for group collaboration.

However, you also want to put stand-up or shift meetings, one-on-ones, lunch with the boss, and company rallies in the mix for team members who don't have access to the virtual tools. You might consider putting communication stations throughout your physical location that include streaming video messages, bulletin boards, and other visual means of sharing information. You can employ mass texting services to alert team members of a new important message at your communication station. You might also develop apps that employees can check to receive information, participate in polls, and so forth.

Finally, get creative with those critical messages—the more visual and interactive, the better. Use humor. Years ago, I got to attend an employee rally at a large hotel. The rally was held three times in two days to ensure all employees could attend, and they repeated the event quarterly. They had messages to share about company updates and reinforcement of core values. The one-hour event included costumes, live music, game shows, funny videos, mock commercials, skits, and dancing. To this day, I can remember the two core values I learned about in that meeting, and I didn't even work there! Perhaps you're not up for orchestrating a production, but even something as simple as taking your email and turning it into a colorful infographic will capture the attention of more people and help your information stand out above the noise.

PROVIDE FREQUENT UPDATES

Consistency is also a key to good internal communication. One of the best examples of company communication I saw during the pandemic came from Edward Brubaker, president and CEO of Living Branches, a senior living organization in southeastern Pennsylvania. As you may well remember, senior living and skilled nursing centers were hit hard by COVID-19, and providing frequent updates to residents, their family members, and employees was of paramount importance. Ed and Alex Metricarti, chief marketing and public relations officer, collected questions from all involved parties and produced an interview-style video that they shared via social media and the organization's live stream channel every week. Alex asked the questions, and Ed answered them honestly and thoroughly. In a very uncertain time, if Ed didn't know the answer, he said so, but as time went on, he had more insights to share. The video was released every Sunday, so family members, isolated elders, and Living Branches team members knew when to expect to hear from Ed. This is an excellent practice, even in the best of times.

Finally, remember that excellent communication is a two-way street. Your employees have information that you don't have because they work closer to your customer. Be intentional about seeking their input and feedback.

INTERPERSONAL COMMUNICATION

Years ago, I was working with a credit union organization with several locations. They were having significant challenges with employee turnover. The human resources department conducted exit interviews, and the overwhelming response was that internal communication had much room for improvement. The leaders of the credit union went to work to provide transparent information through a variety of channels: an intranet, a newsletter, and even video updates featuring the CEO. The turnover issue not only remained, but it continued to worsen. So, they listened deeper and discovered that the problem wasn't about keeping up with the news but about *the way* leaders in the organization talked to their direct reports. They felt disrespected and unappreciated. It wasn't informational. It was interpersonal.

A study of nearly 20,000 employees worldwide, conducted by *Harvard Business Review* and Tony Schwartz,[7] showed that more than half the respondents did not feel respected by their bosses. Considering the boss/employee relationship has long been touted as a key driver in employee retention, it would seem that interpersonal skills and emotional intelligence are critical competencies for anyone in a managerial position.

Here are a few ways you can improve your interpersonal skills.

KNOW THYSELF

One of the critical competencies of any good leader is a high degree of self-awareness and self-regulation. *"Communication,"* says Angie Flynn-McIver, *"is one of those places where the higher up you go, the less feedback you get."* She recommends checking in now and then with someone who's going to give you the straight scoop. Say, *"Here's what I was trying to make happen in this meeting. How did that work? Was there anything that you think hit the wrong note?"* Angie says, *"My favorite questions for a leader to ask their coach or trusted coworker are: 'What did you think I was trying to do? How did you think I was trying to make you feel? What outcome was I looking for?' Then you can start to assess what's working and what's not working in your communication style."*

When you know yourself, you can deliberately show up in a way that's going to support your communication needs as well as everyone else's. Angie offers this example: *"Let's say you're a leader and you go into a meeting all excited about an idea. You present it to the team and begin to get pushback. Now your reaction shows up in your body and your voice, and you default to defensiveness. This can shut down a productive conversation. When you spend time getting to know your own communication style, you can shift into deliberate intention. You can choose not to share the idea until you feel ready. You can share but not ask for feedback. Or, you can go into that meeting remembering what's great about your team and be ready to invite positive contribution and all their different perspectives."*

CONNECT AS A HUMAN BEING

There are a zillion different personality profile tests that can help you determine if you're more relational-focused or task and transactional-focused. However, when it comes to connecting with your team, your customers, and your loved ones, there are two critical levels of communication: human (or relational) and task (or transactional). Recently I was training some call center agents, and we were in the middle of skills practice (a kinder, gentler word for the dreaded *role play!*). In one of the mock calls, the person portraying the caller lamented, *"I need to get into my account, but my house just burned down, and I don't have any of the information you're asking me for!"* The participant portraying the agent went right into task mode, asking closed-ended questions to get her into her account. Do you see where I'm going with this? The caller just said, *"My house burned down,"* and there was no mention of it at all. I had them redo the call and add empathy and a human moment or two before diving into the task at hand. Your team members want you to see them, not as little minions there to do your bidding, but as human beings with thoughts, emotions, and lives outside of work. Make it a practice to check in with your people. Proactively ask how they're doing.

I spoke recently for a hospital system, and the speaker before me was one of their patients. She talked about how disconnected she felt in this world of virtual medicine but then told a story about a simple moment with her physician that made all the difference. Once they completed their medical discussion, the doctor put his chart down, looked into his camera at the patient, and asked, *"So, aside from all this health-related stuff, how are you doing? It's a challenging time out there. How are you handling it all?"* She said that one moment made *all* the difference between feeling like she was just another patient and feeling like her doctor (and, by association, the medical practice staff) truly cared about her. Take a human moment to check in at the beginning and end of your conversations.

SAY THIS, NOT THAT

As we've said, words matter. Take some time to think of some of the words you say by default and positively reframe them. For instance:

> Say this: To avoid this challenge in the future, it might be helpful to. . . .
> Not that: If you had done this, you wouldn't have this problem.

Say this: I want to hear what you have to say. Could we schedule some time later today or tomorrow?

Not that: Don't waste my time. I'm too busy today. You'll
figure it out.

Say this: We're going to try something new, and we're going
to give it our best.

Not that: Oh, it's just another stupid initiative from the home
office.

Say this: We're lucky to have you!

Not that: You're lucky to have a job!

Say this: You're so good with the customers. I heard you helping Mr. Jackson the other day, and he sounded so happy.
You've got a way with people.

Not that: You do a great job.

Did that last one surprise you? Of course, tell people they do
a great job, but follow it up with specifics. Pay attention to your
default language or ask a trusted colleague what they notice.
Then, spend some time turning those phrases around to a more
positive, uplifting bent.

PRACTICE INTENTIONAL WORDS OF KINDNESS

Before my dad passed away of lung cancer in 2012, he spent two
weeks in a hospice house. Four of his five remaining siblings
flew down to Florida to see him. His golfing buddies showed
up to say goodbye. His coworkers from a Publix supermarket
in Bradenton showed up. The first week, Dad was wide awake

and loving it. People told my sister, my mom, and me so many stories about my dad throughout that time. The ones that stood out to me were the ones that were about simple words of encouragement he had given them. A young mother of several children who worked in the produce department wanted to arrange flowers. Dad consistently encouraged her to take a class. She did, and within weeks she was selling more flowers than anyone in the department and was quickly promoted to manager. Another woman had confided to my dad that she didn't think she could keep up with her job in the meat department. My dad would walk by the butcher shop daily and say to her, *"You're so good at this! You're so good at this!"* She said, *"I finally decided to get good at it."* At the time of his passing, she was the assistant manager of the whole store.

Words matter. They have an impact, and we can intentionally choose to positively affect people by encouraging them with our words. In a file cabinet in my office, I have a "smile file." I fill it with notes and email correspondence sent to me by audience members, friends, and others that lift me up and make me smile. It's a great idea to go through the file whenever you're feeling down, and your spirits need a boost. An even better idea is to add to someone else's smile file daily. These can be words you write or words you say, because if the words are meaningful enough to the intended recipient, they will carry them in their heart for a lifetime.

INSPIRATIONAL COMMUNICATION

At its best, our internal communication can inspire people to take action and enable your people to see how *they* make an impact on your customers, their coworkers, the company, and the world. If informational communication is about the head, interpersonal and inspiration are about the heart. If you want commitment from your team, you've got to touch their emotional heartstrings in an authentic way. Here are a few ways you can use communication to inspire.

SHARE SUCCESSES AND FAILURES

As I wrote this chapter, I consistently visited Buffer.com to fill in some of the missing pieces from my research. That's where I came upon Joel Gascoigne's blog post titled "Reflecting on 10 Years of Building Buffer."[8] In the post, he went through the ups and downs of building and running his business throughout its first ten years. Since they default to transparency, he held nothing back, sharing successes but also sharing about cash flow challenges, laying off employees, arguing with and separating from his co-founder, and more. I sat in my office in tears. As a business owner, I've had many of those high highs (happy customers, great team, big successes) and low lows (cash flow challenges, a challenging relationship with a customer, and having to let people go). Reading Joel's blog post assured me that I wasn't alone and inspired me to keep going! When you share your mistakes and your failures as well as your successes, it humanizes you and connects you to your people. When you share what you've been through, you help others to learn from your mistakes. Leaders are sometimes afraid to share that they make mistakes, afraid they'll lose respect or seem weak. Instead, when you share both the ups and the downs, you are seen as authentic, helpful, and human, and that's inspirational!

BREAK BREAD TOGETHER

Guess what? Those employee parties, lunches, and mix and mingles have a purpose beyond fun at work. They break down silos and build bridges. Our Red-Carpet curriculum is highly interactive, whether it's in-person or virtual. We always recommend that our customers put people from different departments together in a session. They start the day off by sitting with the people they know; however, we don't let that stand long. While they always get to go back to their "home base," the participants are up and moving throughout the program and sitting next to someone new for every point of discussion. It's uncomfortable for some at first, but they leave the program with a whole new set of friends—people who work at the same company but with whom they've never had a conversation until that day. Originally, our reason for doing it this way was to break up cliques and keep the program interesting. Our customers, however, told us about another benefit. As one leader put it, *"Silos are crumbling!"* Interdepartmental conversations start to happen when people start to have conversations with people from other departments. (See what I did there?) Stop thinking about the office party as fluffy and unnecessary. Instead, be intentional about those events.

Think about how you'll put different groups of people together and use icebreakers to get people to know one another. You can even do this virtually. For instance, the team at *Buffer.com* uses an app in Slack called Donut to set up "pair calls." If you sign up to use the Donut app, you get paired with a different coworker each week for a thirty-minute call. Buffer provides a list of conversation topics, but typically coworkers (who may be in other countries and have never met) jump on and see where the conversation goes. In one case, a Buffer teammate in Germany jumped on a call with a colleague in Singapore and found that they were both finishing up their coaching certifications. They were strangers before that call, but they now have a podcast together about coaching called Entre Nous.

In at least two studies conducted by professors and led by Jessica Methot of Rutgers University, the researchers found that productivity increases when employees have friends throughout the organization. In their own words, *"Workplace friends influence performance over and above purely instrumental or pure friendship-based relationships."*[9]

CELEBRATE TOGETHER

When my friend Rolinda Stotts gets on a call with me, her very first question is, *"What's your celebration?"* She asks this even when she knows it's been a tough day. It never fails to pull me out of my head and start to focus on what's good in my life and the world. One of the best ways to inspire your team is to celebrate with them. Read positive customer reviews. Share a note that a customer wrote. As we talked about in an earlier chapter, share those Stories Worth Celebrating.™

CONNECT THE DOTS

You also inspire your team by connecting the dots between their job and their impact on the customer and the company. Do this by sharing positive customer reviews, thank-you notes, and organizational successes. Share stories of the impact team members have on the company and have customers speak to employees about the difference in their lives due to their work.

ONE FINAL THOUGHT

Although you may not be as comfortable being as transparent as a company like *Buffer.com*, there is no question that increased transparency and improved internal communication fosters trust between you and your employees. The more they hear it from you, the less they're making up, and the better able they are to do their job effectively. That's a win for everyone!

CHAPTER SIX

Create a Culture in which *Everyone* Is Welcome

On May 25, 2020, the world watched in horror as George Floyd was killed. It was by no means the first murder of a black man or woman, nor, sadly, would it be the last. However, watching that video woke many of us up to the role we play in systemic racism in this country. The tragic event sparked civil unrest and a series of protests in the United States and globally. Leaders in many organizations put out statements in support of antiracism, diversity, equity, and inclusion. One such leader was Mark Ricketts, president and CEO of National Church Residences, a not-for-profit organization that provides full-service retirement communities, affordable housing, and an array of healthcare services and housing for seniors and other vulnerable populations. His statement begins[1]:

> All of us in the National Church Residences family are feeling the shock, pain, and frustration as our nation reels from the tragic murder of George Floyd. There continue to be too

many senseless killings of black men and women and other ugly signs of bigotry and systemic racism.

We need to acknowledge that racism touches the lives of those we love and those we serve—whether that's our co-workers or the seniors in our communities. Racism is a pandemic that must be stopped.

Just as we are fighting hard to stop the spread of COVID-19, **National Church Residences is committed to fighting the pandemic of racism.**

We are a family of employees and seniors of many faiths and many colors. We aspire to do what families do best. Families listen to each other with love and respect. Families have tough conversations. Families do not let others suffer alone.

More important than any statement are the actions that follow. Later in his statement, Mark writes: *"We declare our commitment to helping end racism in our nation, and we also declare our commitment to our core values throughout our organization."* To that end, National Church Residences has formed an antiracism task force and launched the Office of Employee Engagement to focus on culture, leadership, equity, and inclusion.

As I write this chapter, in January 2021, Danielle Willis and Julie Fox are stepping out of their roles of senior vice president of human resources and vice president of education and career development, respectively, to form the Office of Employee Engagement. Says Danielle, *"So often the diversity, equity, and inclusion (DEI) journey is another part of someone else's job or responsibility. The work we've been doing around DEI has been in addition to the rest of our duties and responsibilities."* Before this time, the board of National Church Residences had become engaged in conversations around diversity, equity, and inclusion, and the company had been deliberately looking at culture and employee experience. *"With the results of some employee surveys, a culture audit, and then, of course, the death of George Floyd and our President & CEO's call to action about combatting racism, we determined we wanted to create an office of employee engagement to be more intentional and deliberate about the employee experience,"* reports Danielle. She has been named the senior vice president, employee engagement, and chief diversity officer. She leads the new office, along with Julie Fox, now the vice president of employee engagement and leadership development. Says Julie, *"This investment of a new office with dedicated resources is a statement of how much our organization and leadership are vested in this focus and cultural awareness. Through this commitment, lasting change can be achieved and will not be perceived as solely a training program being offered during a moment in time. This office is connected directly to our President, the board, and our future in terms of the culture we're trying to establish and how we help drive the preferred employee experience. We'll work closely with all departments, leaders, and employees to fulfill our shared vision."*

Coincidentally, the rollout of their employee survey was immediately following the murder of George Floyd, and the leaders at National Church Residences decided to double down and ask more workforce diversity-related questions. Julie elaborates, *"We marketed to our employees that we're intentionally putting in additional questions about workforce diversity, how you perceive that we value differences of opinion, and how employees are treated. That feedback did show there were areas in which there were differences in engagement and favorability among staff. We want to address that and ensure everyone has a similar positive favorable experience. The*

*population of seniors is growing exponentially, and if we don't have
a culture where every individual opinion is valued, then those innovative and creative ideas to solve the problem of providing care and
services and housing are not voiced; the benefits to our mission are
lost."* Currently, the office of employee engagement is made up of
only Danielle and Julie, but they work together with their board
of directors, their CEO, and others in the organization. They
began with an anti-racist task force made up of twelve members,
including frontline employees, that created a charter identifying
focus areas. Says Julie, *"We did not just want this to be a training
program. We wanted a framework that would ensure the work we
were going to do would be impactful and sustainable."* Some of
those focus areas are becoming an ally, education, self-awareness,
minority partnerships, management education, and talent management. There are ten in all. About sixty employees from across
all levels of the organization stepped up to create focus groups
for each area, and that number is growing. Each focus group
has a senior VP or vice president as a sponsor, ensuring this is a
collaborative effort significantly supported by leadership. The ten
groups came together and presented their recommendations collectively to the senior leadership team, and they compiled them
all together into one overarching plan for the Office of Employee
Engagement's work around antiracism.

Some of their early work includes a weekly communication
that goes out to all staff members that provides education around
the history of racism. *"We talked about the fact that the African
American community has a hesitancy around vaccines, and that
stems from a distrust of the health care system,"* elaborates Danielle.
*"We shared information about the Tuskegee Experiment, for exam-
ple."* The Tuskegee Experiment was a study of untreated syphilis

in the African American male, conducted between 1932 to 1972 by the United States Public Health Service. More than half of the 600 men who participated in the study had latent syphilis and were promised free healthcare as an incentive for taking part. However, they were never informed of their diagnosis, given placebos, and intentionally "treated" with ineffective methods. The revelation of this horrendous study has led to a significant distrust of the healthcare system, medical science, and the United States government among the black and brown community.[2] (This is only one of several incidents. Many LGBT seniors, for example, also have a distrust of government or medical systems due to electro-shock therapies and other medical interventions used to rid them of identities and behaviors. Many of these therapies are still legal and used today.)[3] When you add in that many of these folks may also not identify as white, that is just more decades of justifiable distrust.

Danielle continues, *"We also added a piece called 'My Why.' Employees are sending in their reasons why fighting racism is important to them. Some have shared how they grew up during the Jim Crow years or how they are biracial. I shared how my childhood home was spray-painted with KKK. The intent around sharing 'My Why' is that often people will think it's someone they don't know. By peers and coworkers sharing how racism has impacted their lives, it helps with our call to action and the change we wish to make."* Here are a few of those "My Why" submissions, paraphrased for the sake of brevity.

> *"When my daughter was in second grade, she was excited about one of her new friends. One day she came home beyond thrilled that this friend had invited her to her birthday*

party. A couple of days later, she arrived home brokenhearted because this little girl had asked for the invitation back. Her parents had told her she could not invite a black person into their home. So why is my fight against racism important to me? It's because I want my daughter (and all of us) to be able to celebrate the beauty of life together. The bible says that God created us in his image. I'd like everyone to take a moment and consider what that means. It was hard for me to share this personal and heartbreaking illustration of prejudice. I hope that we can all use it as a lesson to help fight the ignorance of racism."

~ LaTasha Banks, property manager

(Lest you think the above story took place in the 1960s, this happened when LaTasha's daughter was seven years old. As I write this in 2021, she is eleven years old.)

"After almost fifteen years of infertility, infant loss, and failed adoptions, my wife and I decided to adopt internationally. Once again, I was confronted with attitudes about race and 'whiteness' that were surprising and disturbing. Racism is a complicated issue. It's something most will admit exists, but few will admit to it. We can see it in a lot of places, but we rarely see it within ourselves.

"This is why, in our home, we fight against racism: *Raising a brown child and watching him struggle to find where he fit into our white world made us all the more committed to creating a life that is filled with diversity. Into our home and lives, we welcome all races, colors, religions, gender identities, and nationalities. Our lifestyle has attempted* to demonstrate our answer to this vitally important question: 'Why?' We are so honored to share our story. We hope that it inspires others to do the same."

> ~ Jim Zippay, corporate chaplain

"My sister is in a biracial marriage, and Jonah is her son. One day, while the news was on and covering the George Floyd tragedy, Jonah took in what he saw, and it terrified him. 'I don't want to be brown! I'm never going outside again!' he cried. It broke our hearts to hear this. No one should have to live in a world where anyone, my nephew included, is afraid to go outside just for being brown. I will never understand how people can treat a person differently because of their skin color. Yes, I am white, and I have not had to deal with this in my life. However, many people I love and care about have to endure this type of behavior, and it breaks my heart.

"Once Jonah calmed down, he decided that when he gets older, he wants to become a great police officer so that he can help 'do things right.' In that single moment, our sweet Jonah saw hope, and he helped me see hope, too!

"I fight against racism because it is important for Jonah to grow up in a world that isn't going to judge him on his skin color. I never thought the world would still be this way in 2020, but it is."

> ~ Lisa Perdue, senior property manager

This is just a sampling of the many stories they sent to me. They all caused me to reaffirm my resolve to be an ally to those who face racism and discrimination.

In addition to the "My Why" statements, president and CEO Mark Ricketts sends out two-minute podcasts and videos called "My Learnings," in which he shares with team members the knowledge he's gained from his reading and research. *"For instance, the first one will be about resistance to vaccines in the black community. Of course, we are providers of affordable housing, so he'll also talk about what he's learned about redlining,"* says Danielle. Redlining is the practice of denying someone insurance, a loan, or a mortgage based on the neighborhood in which they live. Lenders outlined in red, on maps, areas they considered undesirable or riskier when it came to granting loans. Most of these neighborhoods were predominately populated with black or Latino individuals. According to the 1968 Fair Housing Act and the 1977 Community Reinvestment Act, the discriminatory practice is no longer legal. However, there are still many cases of people being turned away for loans because of their race.

Julie acknowledges, *"Obviously, we can't do everything out of the gate. We've started by taking collective information from the assessments, the audits, and feedback from our teams and focus groups, and we're creating a five-year strategic plan that includes baseline measures of success. At the end of the day, we have to show that what we're doing is impacting folks, and they feel as though they have more exposure to opportunities within the organization."*

While the focus, in the beginning, is on racial equity and inclusion, they're using that work to inform where there might be other areas in need of attention within the organization. They've registered for the National Diversity Council Index, an annual measurement of a company's commitment to diversity and inclusion, to assess our strengths and opportunities. *"Once we advance in this area of focus,"* explains Danielle, *"then we'll have a format to ensure that all staff feels they can show up as who they are, their authentic selves. We'll then move into how that manifests for the LGBTQ community, for example."*

Another senior living organization that has embarked on a similar journey is Givens Communities, providing housing and care to elders living in Western North Carolina. In 2014 Givens was going through the CARF® accreditation process through the Commission on Accreditation of Rehabilitation Facilities, an organization that assists health and human services providers in improving the quality of their services. One of the standards relates to diversity, and the HR team realized that beyond their equal employment opportunity (EEO) policy, they didn't have much in place. *"At that point,"* relates human resources director Christian Grunder, *"we created our first committee focused on diversity at the Givens Estates campus."* Givens Estates is one of the organization's four senior living communities. *"The committee came up with two main areas where we would focus our efforts first. They were race culture and the LGBTQ community. We found the SAGECare program, which provides education and consulting, in regards to aging services providers, related to the LGBT older adult community."*

For a year and a half, Givens Communities rolled out education to their team members, achieving SAGECare Platinum Level by engaging 85 percent of their staff in the program. *"It's inspiring,"* adds training and development director Julia McCoy, *"that when we have 580 team members, many of whom are in school or work part-time, that we were able to get that level of participation."*

Sadiya Abjani, director of learning and equity with SAGE, led the sessions. *"I remember those training days,"* she told me. *"It was one of those experiences that, in the end, brought me great joy. They weren't easy, and we had some really tough conversations, but they went through them and ended up just as dedicated."*

One of the challenges Givens faces is generational. Says Christian, *"We serve a generation of people, our residents, for whom the concept of the LGBTQ+ spectrum wasn't the norm when they were growing up."* The organization experienced some pushback from residents and staff members who were uncomfortable with the program. Before being educated, some of the challenges they faced were the inappropriate comments made by both residents and staff regarding team members who are part of the LGBTQ community. *"For instance,"* relates Christian, *"people would tell members of the community, 'I'll pray for you,' not understanding what a hurtful comment that was."* (In essence, you're telling someone that they are wrong as human beings and need your prayers.) *"Or they'd show 'concern' that a child being raised by a coworker in a female-female relationship is not in an appropriate home."*

The Givens Communities leadership, however, was committed to the change. With the help of their employees, they created a respectful workplace philosophy, and inclusion and equity are a big part of that way of being. Says Julia of their commitment, *"What really impressed me is that when we had people make comments that were less than respectful, they were pulled aside and given coaching to help them understand where we are and where we're going. Instead of just letting it go by, we let them know where we stand."* This is important to note because it is the coaching after employees go through any education program that makes the difference in terms of whether the new skills and behaviors stick. *"It was also very powerful for our staff and residents who are part of the LGBTQ community and were on the receiving end of some of those comments,"* adds Julia. During the process, many team members came out as members of the LGBTQ community, either to the group or to Julia and the Givens ministries director, saying how much they appreciated the program. *"They feel comfortable now and tell us they have never worked for an organization that they felt cared about their comfort and inclusion, until now. That tells us we're on the right track."*

Interestingly, while going through the SAGE curriculum, the United Methodist Church, with which Givens is affiliated, took a stand against same-sex marriage. *"Our ministries team had lots of conversations about this. We came to the conclusion that we believe in the work we're doing. We really believe that inclusion is important in every aspect, and we want this to be a safe and welcoming community for everyone."*

Since rolling out the curriculum to their staff, some residents asked to go through the program. Many of their residents have come out as members of the LGBT community, sharing their experience with others. One resident community formed an LGBT support group. People learned to work better together and treat each other with more kindness and respect. At the same time, they gave team members the option to wear a SAGE ribbon on their name badge after going through the program, and the majority accepted. *"We've received a lot of positive comments from visitors, future residents, and staff. It signals, in a subtle way, that this is a safe place, and you are someone I can talk to,"* Christian tells me proudly.

Consider some of the challenges your employees who are part of the LGBTQ community face every day. *"Coming out at work is still a big deal,"* Sadiya Abjani explains. *"I've had multiple people approach me after a session and tell me something to the effect of*

'I take my wedding ring off and leave it in the car because I don't want my coworkers to know I'm married to another woman.' Or 'My child is transgender, but I don't show photos of him. It hurts me because I love my child, and everyone else is displaying pictures of their children.'" Creating an inclusive and respectful environment means fostering a culture where people can show up 100 percent as who they are.

Givens Communities keeps the message in front of people, including celebrating PRIDE week. Residents put up rainbow flags and signs all over the communities, and leaders in human resources gives their team members delicious rainbow cookies with messages of inclusion on them. *"People know that we're staying true to our commitment, even though we've moved on to another topic. We still believe this, it's more than a one-time initiative, and we're going to go through re-certification with SAGECare next year."*

One thing the Givens leadership team knows for sure is that this is an ongoing journey. Says Christian, *"We're not experts by any stretch of the imagination, but we're trying our best to work through these issues. We've had some small successes, but these are challenges we're still working through."* Julia adds, *"We don't want your readers to think we've reached the mountain top. We are very much still on the climb."*

Like National Church Residences and other organizations across the nation, CEO Ken Partin wrote a strongly worded statement about racism following George Floyd's death. It begins:

> I'm writing to you today on behalf of Givens Communities in order to address the blatant systemic discrimination and social inequality our friends, neighbors, and fellow citizens of color continue to face. These issues are here at

our door, and we know many of our residents and team members and their families have been adversely affected by them. The constant reemergence of violent actions against people of color proves that silence is not an option. Now, more than ever, it's important to be courageous and stand up for what's right.[4]

He goes on to elaborate on their continuing work with Dr. Joseph Fox, a consultant, in an effort to become a more inclusive organization. The response to the letter by employees of Givens was immediate. *"We sent it to all team members and all residents and,"* Christian effuses, *"we had team members in multiple departments going to the supervisors and asking, 'Have you seen this letter? Is it for real?' The reply, of course, was, 'Yes, this is what Givens stands for. It's what we're working toward.' I think it gave people hope and a whole new excitement for working here and being part of the team."*

The work is not over; it is just beginning. The conversation on diversity, equity, and inclusion isn't going away, nor should it. It's been a "hot topic" in the human resources field for a while. Indeed, there has been "diversity training" in many workplaces. However, as they discovered at Givens Communities, a one-and-done event is not enough. They had brought in diversity experts in the past to give presentations, but without a straightforward way to move forward and continue the work, the effort died. Says Christian, *"It left our team feeling like 'Well, they did this big push, but we haven't seen anything happen after that so, do they really mean the message?'"*

The truth is that most consultants I talk to know that the work must go deeper to have any lasting impact, but the frustration is that leaders in the companies that hire us want to do the surface work. Diversity educator Jessica Pettitt told me, *"I did what I would like to call old-school diversity training for over a decade, and I was burning out. I wasn't noticing a difference and people just wanted a worksheet. If they had all the vocabulary, they'd be fine, and they could just check it off. It's humiliating to care about something that just becomes a checkbox."* This led Jess to do her own research, which led to her book *Good Enough Now* (Sound Wisdom, 2020 [updated and expanded edition]) and a new way of working that helps people make better connections with themselves and other people across their differences.

Why do the deep work? Well, if you want to create the best employee experience, it must be the best for *all* employees, and the reality is that you won't have an organizational transformation until your people have personal transformations.

There is certainly a business case for becoming a more diverse and inclusive organization. When you bring people with different backgrounds and perspectives into your organization, you open your company to greater innovation and success. According to the Boston Consulting Group, companies with higher-than-average diversity have 19 percent higher innovation revenues.[5]

The more diverse and inclusive your organization is, the better the employee experience. Consider that the workforce is becoming more diverse. A paper called "Unleashing the Power of Inclusion: Attracting and Engaging the Evolving Workforce", written by researchers at Deloitte University and the Billie Jean King Leadership Initiative, shares that the millennial and Generation Z generations are the most diverse in history.[6] Only 56 percent of the 87 million millennials in this country are white, compared to 72 percent of the 76 million members of the baby boomer generation.

In their study, 80 percent of respondents indicated inclusion is important when choosing an employer, and 23 percent had already left an organization for one they deemed more inclusive. So, yes, when it comes to employee recruitment, retention, engagement, and experience, there is a business case to be made for your DEI efforts.

However, if that's your only reason for doing the work, save yourself the trouble. It's not enough. Says Danielle Willis of National Church Residences, *"If we just speak to the fact of a business case that's going to improve your top-line revenue, increase your market, improve employee retention . . . if it's only about a business case, then what you're saying is that I only value your voice and who you are as an individual* as long as it ultimately contributes to my bottom line. *There was, after all, a business case for slavery. I read that in a book, and it literally stopped me in my tracks. If what we're doing is only because we're chasing dollars, then we're going to fail."*

The book Danielle refers to is *Caste: The Origins of Our Discontents* by Isabel Wilkerson (Random House, 2020), and I highly recommend it (something else Oprah and I have in common. Ha!).

Danielle continues, *"I work for a not-for-profit, and I understand, no margin, no mission, but that's not how we're going to change hearts and minds."*

So, yes, it's beneficial to your bottom line to do this work. Don't do it for that reason. Move out of your head and into your heart.

Do it because human beings have a deep-seated need to belong, and you want to help each individual you work with feel included.

Do it because it's more fulfilling to work in a place where people are kinder and more accepting of one another.

Do it because you have the opportunity through your work to bring more compassion and caring to the world.

Do it because you will learn something in the process.

Do it because each individual who works for you deserves to have the absolute best experience.

THE EXPERTS SPEAK

Now that we've talked about the why let's discuss the how. To do this, I tapped into the expertise of the following people:

- Dr. Joseph Fox, EdD, MBA, PHR, owner of Fox Management Consulting Enterprises, in Asheville, NC
- Lenora Billings-Harris, CSP, CPAE, internationally recognized authority on the areas of diversity, inclusion, and bias, author, and founder of UbuntuGlobal
- Jessica Pettitt, MEd, CSP, diversity educator, stand-up comedian, and author of *Good Enough Now*
- Simone E. Morris, CEO of Simone Morris Enterprises LLC, and founder of the Inclusion Bootcamp
- Elaine Pasqua, CSP, diversity and inclusion, workplace culture, sexual harassment speaker and trainer
- Sadiya Abjani, director of learning and equity at SAGE

Let's begin by defining diversity, inclusion, and equity. People often think of diversity as it relates to race or gender, but it simply means different. *"Do you have people on your team who think, speak, and act the same?"* asks Lenora Billings-Harris. *"That would be a homogeneous (or similar) team. Or do you have people who bring different perspectives, a difference of thought, act differently, and look different? That would be a diverse team."* Her question reminded me of a time when I was hiring a project manager for Red-Carpet Learning. We had two incredibly qualified candidates. I liked them both. One of them was quieter and more deliberate. The other was bubbly and upbeat, with a personality very much like the rest of the team and me. I brought another team member into the interview process, and she also liked them both. Of the latter, she said, *"She would fit right in. She's just like us, but do we want someone who's just like us?"* I hired the quieter and more deliberate person, and she was one of the best hires I'd ever made. In fact, we all wondered how we got through without her analytical and systematic thinking. Her differences are precisely what made the team stronger and our services better.

A diverse team can be made up of, but not limited to, people of different genders, ethnicities, orientations, identities, abilities and disabilities, strengths, philosophies, and perspectives.

If diversity is about having different people and perspectives on your team, then *"inclusion is 'who gets to play?'"* Lenora elaborates. *"Many companies have gotten better about the diversity piece, but they aren't so good at inclusion. Then they wonder why there is a revolving door with all the diverse people they've brought on to the team."* Ask yourself, from your diverse team, who gets a seat at the table? Who has a voice in decision-making? Who do you listen to, and who do you involve? Who do you overlook?

"In short," says Lenora, *"diversity is the* who *on the team, and inclusion is who gets to play."*

Equity is about being just, impartial, or fair, or, as Simone E. Morris might say, *"putting your bias at bay."*

Are you ready to begin (or continue) your journey to become a more diverse, equitable, and inclusive workplace? Here are some ideas for you.

AUDIT YOUR DOCUMENTS AND PRACTICES

Start by taking a good long look at your organization. Do you have diversity on your team? If yes, great! If not, read the "Recruit Intentionally" section of this chapter. Before you recruit and hire people with diversity in mind, be sure your culture is ready to be fully inclusive of those people. What are you going to do to make sure your environment is 100-percent welcoming and that everyone will feel included? *"The first step,"* shares Sadiya, *"is to check your company policy and make sure you have a vision and mission statement that includes diversity, equity, and inclusion. Make sure your employee handbook has clear policies."* Dr. Joseph Fox agrees: *"The first thing I do when working with an organization is to look at their historical documents—the website, the employee handbook, and written policies and procedures."* Look not only in terms of racial and ethnic diversity and inclusion, but also gender, sexual orientation, and identity, etc. *"I'll also look at minutes from meetings,"* he continues, *"to see who's in the room, who seems to have the power, who's making motions, and who's involved in the decision-making."*

It's crucial, also, to consider whose eyes are on all these documents looking at verbiage for signs that you might be using exclusive language. Pull in people with diverse experiences and perspectives to make sure you don't miss anything.

KNOW AND SHARE THE HISTORY

One of the challenges we face in being open to different perspectives is that we have a distorted sense of history. As an avid lover of theatre, I attend many productions, and three of the most profound have been performances by actor and playwright Mike

Wiley. The first performance I saw was about the lynching of Emmett Till, a fourteen-year-old boy who was brutally murdered in 1955 for allegedly flirting with a white woman while visiting family in Mississippi. Mike performed every character, and my heart broke throughout his performance for a boy whose name I only vaguely knew and a story I had never really heard about until then. After the performance, Mike took questions from the audience. A white man asked Mike if he was disappointed that only a few people of color were in the audience. A black man in the audience replied, *"We are already well aware of this story. Were you?"* I wasn't. A few years later, I watched Mike's performance of *The Fire of Freedom,* about Abraham H. Galloway, a young slave rebel, an abolitionist, and a Union spy in the Civil War, who later became one of the first black men elected to the North Carolina legislature. Afterward, Mike told us about performing the show for a group of students in North Carolina. He spoke of several young students who were so excited to learn about Galloway and wondered why they had never heard of him. Well, it's because it's not a story that's regularly taught, even in North Carolina.

Mike's mission statement reflects the need for us to know our history to move beyond our fears:

> I do these plays because I believe stereotypes and racism and things of that nature arise from fear—because we are scared of the unknown. When we were children, we were scared of the dark . . . because we didn't know what was in the dark. We thought that box in the corner was a monster because we didn't have the lights on to tell us that it was just a box. But when the lights came on and we saw it was just a box, the fear disappeared. The same logic can be applied to our perceptions of other cultures

or religions, or races. We turn the light on. We figure out
who they are. We learn about them. Then we're not afraid
of them anymore.[7]

If we form our biases because of our unique experiences and
learnings, then, to have a shift in our perspective, it's important
to delve into the historical facts of someone else's experiences
before casting judgment. Says Dr. Joseph Fox, *"In a workshop, I
will typically start with historical context about how violence and
discrimination became so deep-rooted in our history. I will share
examples from 500 years ago about how we had to label people as
inferior so we could justify enslavement and then profit off these folks
and how that created the wealth gap and the educational gap. How
education became the hub of one of the systemic biases that impact
your ability for housing, your ability to participate in the financial
markets, etc. We talk about coming out of the Civil War and the Jim
Crow laws and how we started to see a lot of violence and massacres
throughout the United States. We talk about historical evolution, not
only from a racist point of view but also from a gender point of view.
We discuss that in the United States, women weren't allowed to vote
and that in our early history weren't allowed the right to education."*

Dr. Fox suggests that you start your education with historical
context, using references from sources, such as the Smithsonian
Museum, that most will know are credible. As he shares the
stories, he asks participants to put themselves in the shoes of the
people involved, building empathy. *"The secret piece,"* he shares,
*"is to make sure you don't go in and clobber people over the head so
that they walk out feeling they have been bashed. You want everyone
to feel this is a safe space to start having this discussion."* During a
civic organization presentation, Dr. Fox once noticed an individual in the room, a white male, who was leaning back and not

really embracing the material. Rather than begin with a discussion around race, he began to talk about gender inequality, and ageism, and the importance of value in all of our employees. *"Most men can relate to the experience of how their wives or daughters have felt when they've bought a car or gone to a mechanic and been ignored in favor of talking with the man."* Then we move into the history of racism. By sharing the history, you're planting seeds so that people can build their empathy muscles and see how the experiences that have been, for them, the norm, are also how they've been privileged. *"By the third session, this man was much more receptive. I doubt that we changed all of his thinking, but he was genuinely challenged around the idea of the Confederate flag and Confederate monuments, as he had not realized that the majority of the statues were erected after the Civil War."*

Think about how you could educate yourself, your leadership, and your team around these topics from a historical perspective.

HAVE DEEP DISCUSSIONS

In October 2019, Dr. Denise Caleb, executive vice president of Talent Plus in Lincoln, Nebraska, and her colleagues started to put together a framework to include diversity, equity, and inclusion (DEI) as an intentional part of their business strategy. Their original goal was to partner with another person or organization with in-depth knowhow to better serve their team members and clients. This led to what they call a DEI Think Tank, a cross-functional sector of different employees from different demographics and backgrounds, to come together and start to process, through articles and research in the area of DEI, and go through their own journey of understanding. A team of eight colleagues met two or three times a month, starting in January

2020, to think through identifying partnerships and what to offer internally for employees.

Each day, colleagues gather for what they call Formation. It sets the stage for the day in terms of the focus, based on what they call the Talent Plus Way. They share a core value of the day, provide recognition or what they call Plays of the Day, and focus on what's going well. When they began working remotely, Formation took place online. One of the other cool things you may remember about Talent Plus, if you read my *501 Ways* book, is that they have three floors to their office building, but only one coffee pot. The idea was to ensure that colleagues aren't working in silos and had a chance to bump into each other while grabbing that cup of coffee.

Of course, that experience isn't the same when people are working remotely. Cydney Koukol, EVP, communities, shared, *"The morning after the news about George Floyd, I logged into Formation a bit early. People typically have some casual conversation before it starts. I could just tell that people wanted to talk about what had happened."* She and Talent Plus president Makenzie Rath approached Dr. Caleb and asked her to put something together under the DEI Think Tank umbrella. Explains Dr. Caleb, *"Except for the fact that we were all working from home, we would be getting together to talk about what had happened, whether it was at the coffee pot, or the water cooler, or over lunch, or as we passed each other in the hall."* She put together what she thought would be a couple of intentional formats for colleagues to get together as a company and have some difficult conversations about what was happening. They called the events "Perspective." Says Dr. Caleb, *"It was very intentional to not have that as a plural. We call it Perspective because it's about showing up to provide perspective and gain perspective. We all come from different upbringings, households, and demographics. We've all been taught differently. Then we show up in this complicated environment called work. So, Perspective was a term that resonated with everyone, and it's now become part of the common language of our company."*

What started as a couple of sessions has become a regular part of the Talent Plus experience. The first conversation was scheduled for an hour and went for two and a half hours. Says Cydney, *"Team members shared, cried, and discussed the challenge of racism."* Each gathering begins with what they call their positive regard statement, a set of ground rules to ensure respect and compassion for all who share. For example:

1. They ask that everything shared in the meeting is kept confidential. If a person desires to share someone's story, they must get permission from the person who shared it because "it's not our story to tell."
2. They remind everyone that when they listen and hear, they are bringing courage to the conversation.
3. It's imperative to be courteous and respectful.
4. They talk about embracing the silence. Pauses happen during difficult conversations.
5. They encourage their colleagues to use "I" statements to make sure they *"keep it local."* Dr. Caleb explains to me, *"Keeping it local is keeping it immediate to yourself because my experience, Donna, is not your experience. We're both women, but we are different races, which already means we're having a different experience. We have different intersections depending on whether or not you're a mother, you're married or not, and we're likely having different experiences based on the different communities we have a chance to be a part of, so it's really important to keep it local and immediate."* In other words,

share that this is how *I* feel and don't judge someone else's experience.

6. They encourage people to know that there's the intent of how we want something to land, and then there's the impact of how it lands and to make sure we distinguish between the two.

7. They talk to colleagues about piping up and piping down, encouraging people to share and also reminding the "dominators" to give others a turn.

As of the time I'm writing this, the conversations are facilitated, although Dr. Caleb tells me that may change as time goes on. She will typically begin with two or three conversation starters. It may be adding historical context, as in when their Perspective session focused on Dr. Martin Luther King, Jr., Dr. Caleb recalled, *"We talked about his legacy, and we listened to some of his speeches. Of course, we discussed the 'I Have A Dream Speech,' which was from the March on Washington, an outcome of sanitation workers' unionization efforts to have a safe work environment. However, I wanted to make sure we didn't stop there, so we played the 'If I Had Sneezed' excerpt from his 'I've Been to the Mountaintop' Speech."* This was a speech given by MLK, Jr. one day prior to his assassination on April 4, 1968, in which he described almost losing his life ten years prior when a woman stabbed him after she asked, *"Are you Dr. Martin Luther King, Jr.?"* and he said, *"Yes."* If he had sneezed, he would have died then, as the wound was so close to his aorta. Dr. Caleb continued, *"Then we listened to Robert Kennedy, Jr. announce Dr. King's death, and you could hear the gasp from the audience in the old footage."*

In the instance above, they began with historical context before diving into the discussion. During another session, the topic was interracial relationships. As a perspective starter, they invited a couple to share their story. The wife was Caucasian, and the husband was African American, and *"it led to this really beautiful conversation about the husband's journey, learning his heritage and finding some of his birth relatives. People were so engaged and enthralled with their story. They shared things that have happened to them as a couple because they are experiencing their marriage very differently"* (than two individuals of the same race). Other topics they've explored include democracy and education. They did another in June 2020 to celebrate the LGBTQ+ community and the historic legislation covering and giving protection and rights to the transgender, gay, and lesbian population.

I asked Dr. Caleb what the outcomes of this effort have been. She replied, *"What's happened is that our colleagues love it! They've been very receptive, and they want more. If we could have a Perspective conversation every week, they would love it. They show up, they listen, and they want to know what they can do to put it into action. While I know we'll suggest more actions to take later, for now, we're encouraging people to be aware of inclusiveness, inviting people into their groups, and that 'if you hear something, say something, do something, and listen.' At this point, we only want to give them basic actions to focus on. Some people think you need to march or put yourself into a situation where you're fighting for the cause. Yet, there are other ways to help. You can write your Congressperson, and you can have a voice, you can support and mentor, and you can be an ally for someone."*

The Talent Plus DEI Think Tank also started DEI learning pods, limited to eight people, who go through a seven-week curriculum. They meet for two hours a week, for seven weeks, and explore topics such as blind spots, intersectionality (the idea that people occupy more than one identity position and can be both in a position of privilege and marginalized), and microaggressions. *"We have them work on their own statement around their intersections. It's very self-reflective,"* Dr. Caleb explains.

If there's one thing that all the experts agree on, a one-and-done diversity training program will not create the shift you're looking for. It's time to have the tough conversations. The one way to really understand someone else's perspective is to listen to their experience. Inclusion expert Elaine Pasqua suggests, *"When we sit down, and we talk to one another, we break through all of those barriers and walls, and we get to know each other. Organizational leaders can launch a conscious effort to raise awareness. Ask what are people with disabilities experiencing? What are Latinx and Asian people experiencing? What kind of hurtful things are people of color experiencing? Foster an understanding that we all have something important to bring to the table."*

Lenora Billings-Harris adds, *"We can't assume anymore that people aren't going to talk about politics and religions and the issues of the day at work because they are. Instead of having it off the table, put it on the table, and address some of the things that are a challenge in the workplace for them."* Lenora has the following suggestions for leaders who want to go deeper in their discussions.

- Before you attempt such conversations, be very clear on your written policies and procedures about respect in the workplace. Remind people of those policies and the expected behavior.
- Create a safe space. Tell the group, *"We're going to talk candidly about what's getting in the way of our being our most productive with one another."*

- Assure people that you're not here to attack their faith or beliefs. In the end, there will still be differences of opinion. The agreement will be about how to create a more respectful, civil, and compassionate work environment.
- Leaders can pose questions and get people talking.
- Encourage people to frame their statements in this way: *"When people say this, this is how I feel."*
- When people bring up concerns outside of work, simply say, *"I understand that may be happening. How can we build a more respectful work environment?"*

Dr. Denise Caleb, who, in addition to her role at Talent Plus, has been facilitating DEI conversations for more than sixteen years, adds, *"It's important to understand where your culture is before starting. At Talent Plus, we already had a framework for how we show up respectfully for one another. We've already been talking for years about listening and really hearing people, so we were a little ahead of the game to bring something like this into the work environment. This work is really about transformation and change management, so you want to make sure you've got the right pace and are introducing the right levels of change. Otherwise, you will overwhelm people if you're moving too quickly. If your organization is on letter C and you try to take them all the way to Z overnight, then you're going to get a lot of pushback because they're not going to be able to digest that level of change."*

Before diving into the deep conversations, a best practice would be to enlist the help of an outside expert, or an experienced person on your internal team, to take the process one step at a time. Keep in mind, however, that the one-and-done training model will not produce the outcomes you desire.

BE READY TO ADDRESS THE FEAR

The reason why most organizational leaders want a list of vocabulary words and some sound bites about diversity, and to be able to check the box that they completed training, is that having those deep discussions gets messy. Everyone comes to the table with their preconceived notions and fears. You have to be prepared to hold space for and address all those fears. Lenora Billings-Harris tells me of a time when she was working with a large technology organization. As part of her process, she did one-on-one interviews with everyone on the leadership team and group sessions with all of the employees.

During one of those one-on-one interviews, a gentleman, who had risen through the company, had huge bottom-line responsibility, and reported directly to the CEO, asked her a question. He said, *"I know I'm well regarded here, but as a white, middle-aged man, what chances do I have in today's environment? This company is so focused on hiring more women that I don't feel like I really have a chance. I also don't know how to coach my white male employees."* Lenora, who was honored that he felt safe enough to share these feelings, replied, *"First, know that I can easily see that you are very good at what you do. However, you now realize that some of the opportunities you've received came easily to you because you are a white man. There were people who saw your potential and mentioned your name in rooms when you were not in the room, which created opportunities for you. In today's environment, your name should still be brought forward, but along with the names of others. The bottom line is that yes, it's going to be more competitive and harder than it was before, but you can coach your mentees to be very, very good at what they do. When their name is brought forward as a slate of five unique people,* they will sometimes *be the best choice. What will give you the edge is to get more comfortable interacting with people different than you. That focus on understanding the benefits of diversity will give you a competitive advantage."*

It's also important to recognize that many people will fear that you're asking them to give up long-standing belief systems or their religious faith. For instance, knowing that I work with many faith-based organizations whose religious doctrine varies when it comes to the LGBTQ community, I asked Sadiya Abjani how she reconciles this with her clients. She was excited by the question. She said, *"Yes! We work with a ton of religiously affiliated organizations. The first thing to know is that you can't automatically assume that because an organization is religiously affiliated, they aren't going to be LGBT welcoming. That's false."* (Yet another bias.) Sadiya, who identifies as queer, continues, *"Secondly, I'm very religious. I'm Muslim. When I share that with participants, they are always a little shocked, and they think, 'Well, with all the false negatives we've heard about Muslims, if she can do it, then we can.' Finally, if your faith is not supportive of the community, and you don't believe that identifying as an LGBT community is right, that's fine. I'm not going to take that away from you. But let's put it aside for a moment and focus on your desire to provide the best care for the people you serve and the best experience for your coworkers and your team. In order to do that, there are absolutely things you need to know that we're going to cover in this four-hour course, so you can create the best experience possible. If that's the goal of this organization, then let's focus on how to be respectful of everyone regardless of personal opinions."*

We can disagree and still be respectful, kind, and caring. Understand, though, that another fear that will come up in these conversations is the fear of "being changed" or having to turn away from one's faith.

When it comes to topics like diversity, inclusion, and equity, the fears are deep, and they are real. Validate the fears of each person in the room, and then continue the conversation so you can move past them.

REPRESENT

Almost all of the experts I interviewed talked about doing an audit of the materials and verbiage used to represent the organizations they worked with. In the course of producing custom training videos for our clients, the team at Red-Carpet has occasionally had to remind leaders to ensure their videos were inclusive and representative of their team members. Since we use their people as stars of the video, we remind them to invite people of all colors, genders, generations, and positions to be part of the show. When I look at some websites, the pictures sometimes showcase mostly white people. You may think, *"Well, those photos represent our customers. They are mostly white."* Understand that may be true, but when people visit your website and they don't see themselves, they may not feel welcome. Representation matters, especially when it comes to creating an inclusive employee experience.

RECRUIT INTENTIONALLY

Perhaps your team lacks diversity, and you've thought, *"We just don't get applicants that reflect the level of diversity we desire to have."* It's time to get more intentional about your recruitment and hiring process. Simone E. Morris agrees: *"I've come across potential clients who tell me that 'In our industry, it's hard to find diverse talent.' When I get curious about their recruiting approach, I discover more often than not that they have not stretched themselves to diversify where they find the talent they are seeking."*

Lenora Billings-Harris adds, *"To have more diversity of thought, rather than groupthink, means you have to look at your recruiting practices. Are you looking in different places so you can surface the talent that's right for you, or do you get comfortable going to the same places all the time? Even universities have certain philosophies, so if you recruit from only one university, you're not tapping into diversity of thought. For instance, if you're a technology company and you only take applicants from Stanford or MIT, you're missing out on incredible talent that may come from lesser-known universities."*

Is it time to shake up your recruiting practices? Is it time to expand the pool of people who get mentored and groomed for leadership positions? Only you know the answers to these questions.

BEWARE THE LABELS AND MICROAGGRESSIONS

Recently, I asked one of my best friends his thoughts about humor on television and perceptions related to being gay. He said that one of the things that bothered him the most is when people think they know him because he's gay. I recalled his response when I asked Sadiya from SAGECare if she had anything to add, and she replied, *"The one final thing I would say is that it's important to remember that a person's LGBTQ identity doesn't overwhelm their other identities. One person's experience is going to be different from another person's experience."* We're all individuals with our unique stories, regardless of race, gender, abilities or disabilities, orientation, or whatever other label others see or think of first. This brings to mind a quote from the stage production and film *In & of Itself* and said by actor and writer Derek DelGaudio: *"I'm not defined by what you see. I'm also defined by all the things you will never see."*[8]

Beware also of microaggressions, those things we say and do that may be hurtful to others. Examples of these are saying *"You people," "You're so articulate"* (because you assumed they wouldn't be), *"Is that your real hair?," "Where are you from?"* (because you're assuming someone is foreign-born), *"You're gay? Oh, you should meet my gay friend Alice,"* or, to a disabled person, *"I could never overcome it as you have!"* Telling a woman to *"smile more"* and talking over the women in the room are microaggressions. I would even venture to say that "male-bashing" would be another form. Before you sigh and think, *"Ugh! Now she wants us to be perfectly politically correct!"* I invite you to rethink that term and consider this your opportunity to be empathetic and considerate of another person's feelings.

BECOME AN ALLY

Once the team at Givens Communities went through their educational experience, they were offered the opportunity to wear a ribbon denoting their support of the LGBT community. The majority of the team members wear them on their name badges. Prospective residents and employees have commented and said, *"I see that on your badge, and I appreciate it. It's a subtle way that you tell me 'It's a safe place to be and that you're someone I can talk to.'"*

Elaine Pasqua shares, *"We have to be willing to be allies to others in the workplace and call others out on their behavior. Not in a confrontational way, but from the perspective of empathy, and sharing privately how the words or behavior you witness may have hurt the individual in question."* Understand that the recipients of discrimination often don't speak up because they are already feeling like an outsider, and by speaking up they fear increased or continued alienation. You can help by standing for people and not being complicit by staying silent.

If you're truly going to be a place that embraces diversity and equity and creates the most inclusive environment, then you have to stand for people where it counts. The time will come where you're going to be asked to draw a line in the sand. Lenora Billings-Harris shared the story of a hospital she worked with where they were struggling with the biases of some of their patients. Some people were refusing to be treated by a black doctor. They checked their policy and had everyone on the team role-play their response to that situation. For instance, they were taught to say, *"Dr. Cutting is not only the doctor on duty, but she is the best qualified for your condition. If we were to bring in someone else, you would not be getting the best care."* If they still refused, then they would say, *"We will happily transfer you to another hospital."* Another Fortune 100 company had a customer who repeatedly told homophobic jokes. They knew by talking with him they could lose a multi-million-dollar account, but they told him, *"We protect the environment our employees work in."* The client stopped, and they did not lose the account, but it was a real possibility that they would, and they stepped up anyway.

Says Lenora, *"This is where the character of an organization comes in. Are you saying this is what you want only when it's easy? Or are you saying this is the culture you want, period?"*

OWN YOUR OWN STORY

In an earlier chapter, I shared a story about hearing Jessica Pettitt speak at the National Speakers' Association convention. It was a four-minute and thirty-seven-second speech that had a huge impact on me.[9] I had a chance to revisit the topic with her in preparation to write this book, and she elaborated: *"It's not about refraining from making judgments and assumptions. Of course, you're going to, because you want to feel safe and prepared. However, own your own story and own the habits and experiences that helped you create that story. Realize that the story you are writing about someone else is something they had zero participation in. They had zero input into your first draft of that story. That's why printing that first draft out triple space, with extra-wide margins matters, because you're talking your truth. That's not a value judgment. It is your truth, but it's not necessarily accurate, and it doesn't have anything to do with the other person unless you ask them in a curious, gener-ous way to tell you their story. Leave room for edits in your story and make them by listening and engaging with others."*

If we could all remember that our beliefs and opinions are shaped by our own experiences, that others have lived their lives with different experiences, and get curious about one another, the world would be a better place. Here's a little of how the story I've written about people has changed through the years.

I grew up in the small town of Westport, Massachusetts. Most of the people in the neighborhood, including our family, were Catholic. There was one Protestant family across the street. My sister and I were friends with the children in that family, but we had our stories about their religion and they had their stories about ours. Many of my friends and schoolmates were first-generation Americans, born to parents who came to the United States from Portugal. I enjoyed the food, the colors, and the vibrancy of their culture, and yet I readily used a derogatory term for immigrants who came to our town. It was a popular term among my peers, and none of us thought anything of it. I didn't think of it as being mean; it's just the way everyone talked in that area at that time. My mom tells me about a time when I saw a black woman in line at the bank and squealed with delight, *"Mom! It's Julia!"* Our neighborhood, our church, and my school were full of white people, and until that point the only black person I had seen was Diahann Carroll, who played Nurse Julia on television. I also had a Julia Barbie doll, but that was the extent of my experience. Somewhere along the line, I picked up the idea that you had to lock your doors when driving through a "black neighborhood." I had an aunt who had Down syndrome and with whom I spent much time as a girl. It's a big reason I'm very comfortable around people with intellectual and developmental disabilities, became a special needs camp counselor, and taught theatre to adults with Down syndrome earlier in life. Like many of us, I grew up using the word *gay* in an insulting way, even before I knew what it meant. Once I did know the meaning of the word in terms of a human being's orientation or identity, the idea was foreign to me, and I was not always kind in my conversations about it. None of this is to say that I was a bad person. I was simply a young girl, growing up with certain experiences that shaped my worldview.

When I left for college and the aforementioned Renaissance Faire, I met different people. My friends included people of color. One of my dearest friends came out to me as gay. We had family members come out as members of the LGBTQ community. I was meeting people from outside my small-town bubble. My friends were made up of people who followed a variety of different faiths, including Judaism, Catholicism, other forms of Christianity, Buddhism, Islam, and New Thought. I became friends with (*gasp!*) Yankees fans. As a result of my experiences as a young adult, my story received some serious edits.

I'm still rewriting as I identify needed edits to my own narrative drafts.

Recently one of my friends from the Renaissance Faire acting troupe, a black man, reminded me of the time when the Ku Klux Klan was in Lancaster County, Pennsylvania, where we were living and working. He told me he had been terrified and that he didn't think the rest of us noticed the signs about a KKK rally posted all over Lititz. He was right. I remember talking about it and that we had a slight fear that they may show up at the Faire. Honestly, though, it didn't even occur to me how scared my friend must have been and how we needed to protect him. I had a vague sense that they were in town, but my friend was right: I did not notice the signs. Another rewrite of my story, understanding now that I must become aware and be an ally to people in marginalized communities.

A few years ago, I was called out on a speaking evaluation for using hetero-centric language, meaning excluding people of the LGBTQ community. As someone who feels she is an ally to that community, I took the comment very personally and ran around to all my gay friends looking for affirmation. In the end, I changed the wording of that particular illustration in my speech and strived to ensure my language is all-inclusive going forward—another rewrite of my story.

Clearly, I could go on and on and on. Even today, I recognize biases that I hold about people who think differently from me. When I decide to get curious enough, the stories I'm telling myself today will be rewritten as well. Because here's the reality: Our truth is just that. It's *our* truth. It's shaped by our experiences and what we do or don't allow ourselves to get curious about. They are stories that make us feel safe and comfortable, but the stories aren't necessarily accurate. My message is *not* that you should have the same perspective as I do. Nor do we have to change our core beliefs or agree with anyone. Rather, that it would behoove all of us, in this world of great division, to step out of our comfort zone, ask questions, listen to the answers, and, as Jessica Pettitt would say, *"leave room for edits."*

In the course of a conversation, I asked Danielle Willis, senior vice president of the Office of Employee Engagement for National Church Residences, what their work around diversity, equity, and inclusion meant to her as a black woman. Here's how she replied: *"At a recent senior leadership retreat, I was sitting around the table with my peers, and I shared with them that they're giving me hope. It may seem simple, but seeing our CEO Mark's call to action and our public commitment, I said to my peers that they have just committed to ensuring that I have a voice. That I, as a black woman, have a voice in this organization as well as outside of this organization. So, for me, that's what it is, and that's what their commitment means to me, and they have instilled a real sense of hope."*

To put employees first, and create the best experience for your team members, do the deep work, the real work, and commit to creating a culture (and a world) where everyone is welcome.

CHAPTER SEVEN

Get Creative with Compensation

On March 21, 1964, in Waterloo County, Ontario, Canada, twenty-two Mennonites put one dollar each into a cash box. That's how the Waterloo County Mennonite Credit Union was born. Founder J. Winfield Fretz saw a connection between the underlying structure of a credit union and the Anabaptist Mennonite values of a commitment to peace, social justice, and mutual aid. In 2016 they rebranded as Kindred Credit Union but remained committed to their purpose of inspiring peaceful, just, and prosperous communities.

So, it's incomplete alignment with that philosophy that Kindred Credit Union has committed to paying their team members a living wage. According to their website, *"A living wage is the hourly wage a worker needs to earn to cover their basic expenses within their community, such as food, clothing, shelter, and transportation. It also includes medical expenses, recreation, and a modest vacation. It's a wage that allows employees not just to subsist but also to have access to the types of things that make for a decent quality of life: the ability for a family to participate in the community and be healthy and active social citizens.*"[1] Pamela Hillis, manager, staff experience at the credit union, had developed an interest in the living wage movement growing in pockets of the country. She brought it to the attention of their CEO at the time, Brent Zorgdrager, who bought into the idea immediately. Says Pam, *"For many companies, it's the HR department that starts talking about it, and they have the job of getting senior leadership on board. We were fortunate that our CEO was in alignment with our thinking."* In 2013, Kindred, along with eleven other organizations, became founding members of Living Wage Waterloo Region. They later combined with other Ontario Living Wage networks to incorporate as Living Wage Canada. While Pam's involvement started initially as part of her role at Kindred, she's now personally involved as chair of Living Wage Waterloo Region and a board member of Living Wage Canada.

Working with their network, they were able to determine what they believe to be a proper living wage for the Southwest Ontario region. They also developed a certification process to enable employers to phase in their implementation. Kindred Credit Union has earned their Champion Level, which means they pay all full- and part-time employees and regular contractors a living wage as defined by Living Wage Canada. It also means they are committed to raising wages as the living wage is recalculated.

"Admittedly," explains Pam, *"it wasn't difficult for Kindred to get to a place where we were paying all our staff a living wage."* She encourages those who are concerned about taking the leap to consider how they will save on recruitment and turnover costs. *"Even staff engagement improves. When your employees are able to take care of their health, and they aren't worried that they can't pay their rent or for their next meal, you have less absenteeism and*

less presenteeism." *Presenteeism* is the term given to a situation in which the employee is present physically, but not "fully there" or fully productive because of injuries, health-related conditions, and other worries.

Across Ontario, the network now has 350 member companies, and it's growing. This excites Pam! *"The larger we can build this network where more and more companies are paying a living wage, the more we can support some of those in traditionally low-paying fields like food service, or cleaning companies, or security. If you have a whole bunch of living wage employers like Kindred, who are willing to pay a premium to have a cleaner that pays a living wage, then it allows that cleaning company to become more successful and afford higher wages."* The organization has its sights set on enrolling some of the largest employers across Canada. *"That's where we can have a real impact. The larger the employer, the more staff, the bigger impact they have on people's lives."* Pam cites the Living Wage Foundation in the UK as an inspiration. They grew from a grassroots effort in London into the largest living wage network in the world, with just under 7,000 employer members dedicated to paying fair wages.

The movement is growing in countries all over the world, including the United States. Rebecca Smith, Kindred's vice president, engagement and values, hypothesizes, *"There's just the general rise of social conscience that's happening in societies. For instance, we were pioneers in the space of socially responsible investing, and now you see more and more people doing the same."* No surprise that Kindred Credit Union is also a Certified B Corporation, joining the ranks of such companies as Ben & Jerry's and Patagonia, which are committed to using the power of business to solve social and environmental problems.

In terms of paying their own staff a living wage, Frank Chisholm, director, brand, and marketing for Kindred, says, *"Our members would expect no less of us because our whole value set is to support each other in community. Part of our purpose is to inspire peaceful, just, and prosperous communities, and that fits and aligns completely with the notion of paying a living wage."*

The minimum wage in Ontario, as of February 2021, is $14.25, and Living Wage Canada calculates a living wage in the Waterloo region as $16.35 per hour.[2] (The minimum wage would translate to $11.19 US dollars, and the living wage would be $12.84 US dollars.) As a citizen of the United States, I have to admit I was shocked to discover how far behind we are. As this chapter is being written, the minimum wage in the United States is $7.25 per hour. According to the calculator developed by Dr. Amy K. Glassmeier, a living wage in North Carolina, where I currently make my home, is $15.26. That's a long way to go.

Let's look at a little history.

In November 2012 hundreds of fast-food workers in New York held a strike to demand better pay. This sparked a national debate in the United States about raising the minimum wage. A few years later, more than 60,000 low-wage workers in over 200 cities across the United States lined the streets protesting the federal minimum wage (which has been $7.25 since 2009) and calling for a new national minimum of $15 per hour. These marches sparked similar protests internationally in countries like Brazil, Japan, New Zealand, and the United Kingdom. In June 2014, the city of Seattle, Washington, made history when it became the first in the United States to mandate a $15 per hour minimum wage for all workers, and in 2019 the US House of Representatives passed a bill to raise the federal minimum wage to $15 by the year 2025. As of February 2021, no such bill has been passed by the Senate, although as I write this chapter it's under active discussion in the Biden administration.

Opponents of the wage hike argue that it will result in employees working fewer hours, increased unemployment, and higher prices. Still, it's a conversation that isn't going away. Like it or not, employers are going to have to increase compensation for their lowest-paid employees sooner rather than later. For one thing, we have a whole lot of hourly workers who have woken up to the fact of just how essential they are. People are placing more importance on work-life balance, and when you have to work two or three jobs to feed your family, that's an impossible task. How many of you found that when you could put your furloughed employees back to work in 2020, they preferred to stay on unemployment because it paid them more than their actual jobs?

While I absolutely believe that *everyone* should be offered the chance to earn a good living that easily takes care of their basic and quality of life expenses, I understand that it's complicated. Most of the people I speak to about this topic want to pay their people more money; they just don't know how to do it in a sustainable way. There's no easy answer and, even if there were, this author is not the one to provide it. Just ask my bookkeeper, my husband, and anyone who has ever worked for me. Money matters have not been my strong suit. However, how could I write a book about putting employees first without addressing the subject of compensation?

Instead of offering you advice, I give you the perspective, experience, and creative thinking of those in other organizations who have found a way to pay their people fairly. Your organization is unique, so I'm not suggesting that you do exactly as these organizations have done. Instead, my hope is that by reading their stories, you will be more open to the possibility that there is an answer that will work for your company and your people. Fair warning: A couple of these ideas are revolutionary, but that may be just what it takes to get you thinking more creatively about compensation.

RAISE WAGES AND LOWER TURNOVER

Whenever a team of senior leaders calls us at Red-Carpet Learning to discuss working with them to improve their company culture, the conversation invariably turns to their desire to minimize employee turnover. When asked how much turnover they have, they can generally be specific with a percentage. When we ask them, however, how much money that turnover is costing them, they don't know. They've never done the math. It makes you wonder how much money could be found if you tightened up financial waste, such as lost productivity and the costs of employee turnover. Says Chuck Gallagher, a vice president with American Funeral Financial, *"It's an analytic exercise. Have you done the work to discover what's it costing you to train people? What does it cost you to hire people? How long does it take for an employee to become productive? The question most companies face is that if we go ahead and bit the bullet, and pay our people more, does it change anything? Will we still have turnover?"*

American Funeral Financial acts as an intermediary between a family who's lost a loved one and a funeral home providing a service to that family. They verify the family's insurance policy and fund it immediately, using the policy as collateral to advance payment to the funeral home, and the family has access to cash.

The company was started in 2009 and was sold to a public enterprise in 2014. They have in excess of 100 employees.

"When we began," explains Chuck, *"it was an employer's market. Being able to hire someone at $10 or $11 an hour was fairly easy. Over time, the unemployment rate (in the United States) went down dramatically, which means we had to work harder for quality talent. By 2018 the job market was at about 3.5 percent, and we were concerned about finding people. Then when we were able to find them, we could start at a lower rate, but in reality, by the time they're trained, would it not have been better to have compensated a little higher on the front end so the compensation and benefits package was something that would cause someone to rethink leaving?"*

By the end of 2019, wages had been raised to a minimum of $15 per hour. At that point, employees were working out of one of two office buildings the company had in South Carolina and Alabama. Now the American Funeral Financial employees are working from home, wearing what they want to wear, and making a good wage. Productivity went up 20 percent, and annual turnover went down dramatically. *"We only had three people out of 100 leave, and seven actually came back from other places because now they can work from home, get paid a better wage with wonderful benefits, and they're happier."*

It may be true that not every organization may be able to cover the cost of higher wages by lowering turnover. The question is, however: Do you even know what your employee turnover is costing you? What about lack of productivity? Are you stuck on keeping those expensive corporate offices now that you know people can work from home? Where else might you be leaking money that could be parlayed into providing a fair wage for your people? These are questions that deserve some answers.

PAY FOR PERFORMANCE

"Let's let go of the old adage that everyone gets a merit wage," advises Elliot Dinkin, president and CEO of Cowden Associates, Inc. *"It's okay if a high performer gets a 4- or 5-percent raise and some people, the low performers, get zero. You're better off paying your high performers more and not worrying about the others if they aren't necessarily going to come around."* One of the problems with across-the-board raises, according to Elliot, is that eventually there is a cap on what you can pay for certain positions. You're also losing money by rewarding people who are not pulling their weight in the organization. The pay-for-performance model he suggests is not always embraced by managers. Not only does it mean you've got to have difficult decisions with your team members, but as a leader, you're being evaluated on the value your team brings to the company.

The consultants at Cowden Associates, Inc., based in Pittsburgh, Pennsylvania, work with employers who want to be certain they have in place the ideal combination of compensation benefits and retirement plans to be competitive, cost-effective, and compliant. Elliot offered his insights for leaders who want to raise wages for their hourly employees.

Not only is Elliot a proponent of merit raises, but he also stresses that the goal should be to move your lowest-paid workers up as quickly as possible. You don't necessarily have to promote everyone to a leadership position, but rather make it very clear through a transparent career ladder of sorts how they can move through the organization to earn additional compensation. Employees who are better trained and who stay longer are more valuable to the organization. Cowden Associates also advocates looking at total compensation rather than only focusing on wages. What can you offer in terms of flextime, retirement contributions, extra life insurance, additional time off, or other meaningful incentives? For organizations looking at raising the minimum wage for their hourly workers, Elliot cautions, *"When you raise the bottom of the pay scale up, you've got to think about everyone in the organization. What's the incentive for being a supervisor if that person is suddenly making only 50 cents more than someone in an entry-level-position?"* This is where focusing on a total compensation package comes in handy. You may not be able to raise salaries for managers as you lift your low-paid workers up to a living wage, but you can offer other benefits that are meaningful to them.

"It's also time to leave behind the one-size-fits-all philosophy when it comes to benefits," Elliot recommends. *"When I'm twenty-four years old, you can't tell me you have the greatest 401(k) plan in the world because I don't care. I need cash now. I'm getting married and having babies. On the other hand, don't tell me at forty-five years old that your biggest benefit is paying off student loans."*

Are you churning through low-wage employees rather than showing them a clear path to success and helping them become more valuable to your company? Are you stuck in old ways of thinking? Perhaps it's time to bring your compensation strategy into the 21st century.

A TRANSPARENT FORMULA

As you've already learned, Buffer.com is passionate about transparency, including when it comes to their salaries. They also have a very specific formula, which they make public and have tweaked over the years. Head of public relations Hailley Griffis admits, *"I have a hard time imagining working somewhere that isn't at least somewhat transparent with their salary formula, having had this experience with Buffer, especially knowing the gender pay gap."* Even in 2021, female executives in the United States are *still* typically being paid only 82 cents to every dollar earned by a man.[3] That number is even less for women of color. That's just another reason why having a transparent formula for how you compensate your employees is a good idea. Buffer starts by benchmarking specific roles, based on salaries in the San Francisco market, times a cost-of-living multiplier, depending on where an individual resides. Then, employees move through levels and steps to increase their wages or salaries. There are six levels for most positions, and each level has four steps on which team members are evaluated.

As an example, one position is graded on ownership and initiative. In step one, an entry-level person has no ownership and receive instructions on all tasks. They are not expected to take initiative and will do work as directed. In step four, entry-level employees have taken on increasing ownership and can work independently on many tasks. They are also increasingly taking the initiative by asking targeted questions. Explains Hailley, *"The steps are not a 'progress bar' and are not necessarily meant to be a strictly linear progression. A teammate could potentially advance multiple Steps at once. A change in Step can happen at any time through each area director's discretion and requires no approval or discussion outside of the area."*

The company makes their formula, their levels and steps system, and a spreadsheet of their team members current salaries/wages available to the public. There's even a calculator where you can figure out your starting pay were you to work at Buffer.com. You can find links to these resources and more by going to www .RedCarpetLearning.com/EmployeesFirstResources.

COMMISSION-BASED PAY

Let me re-introduce you to Chad Mackay, the CEO of Fire & Vine Hospitality, the parent company to a series of fine dining restaurants and lodging across the Pacific Northwest. In 2014, when Seattle raised the minimum wage to $15 per hour, Chad could see the writing on the wall. The company was already paying higher wages than many of their competitors, and with tips, servers were averaging $50–60 in tips. While many states raising the minimum wage have a tip credit—meaning the restaurant could pay a lower wage plus tips—Washington state does not. Chad could see that at the rate his company was growing, a base rate of $15 per hour for servers was unsustainable. He'd be out of business in seven years or fewer.

He pulled his senior servers together, and for about six months, they held roundtable discussions. Chad explains, *"When we make decisions, we have three criteria. Is it great for the guest? Is it great for our team? Is it financially sustainable? I told the servers, whom I consider my best salespeople, that someone else had made a decision that affected us, and it was not going to be financially sustainable. Nor would it be great for the employees or the guests. When you run a restaurant, you want your team to show up at 4 o'clock. Guests start arriving at 4:45 pm, giving you time to do line-up, taste menus, and do staff education updates. With minimum wage being so high and not having tip credit, we eliminated that as a standard practice to save money."*

As a team, they started analyzing the data and the problem and came up with the concept of commission, by which you can have a base wage that is different from the state minimum wage. The idea was to implement a service charge for every guest check and use it to pay servers a commission on top of their base wage. The servers in the working group said, *"We'll give it a roll because we want us to be successful, and we trust you."* The servers asked for two things. Rather than pool all the commissions and split them across everyone, they wanted to be paid on individual performance. Second, they wanted to be allowed to get a bump if there were guests who wanted to tip in addition to the service charge. Chad agreed, with the stipulation that there would be no begging for tips. It would be evident to guests that tips were appreciated but not expected, and if the servers started begging, he would take tips away. *"It's a privilege, not a right."* It's worked. Senior servers make it very clear to new employees that they are not to mess up the system.

The results? The average server started making 10–15 percent more under the new plan than with the old method, making $60–$70 an hour in base wages, commissions, and tips. It's been easier to recruit good people, and turnover has been significantly less. While they lost a few guests who didn't care for the service charge, most appreciate it, and the company has grown since. The commission-based approach has given Fire & Vine Hospitality staff the ability to make extra money, and the company grew revenues and profits.

This approach may or may not work for you. However, I hope you will take away that Chad worked *with his staff* to come up with the idea that worked for them.

INDEPENDENT CAPITALISM

Raised by two successful entrepreneurs, Gabriel Menegatti from San Paulo, Brazil, has been one himself since he was fourteen years old. He's been very successful and made a lot of money. He started his latest company—or team, as he prefers to call it—in 2012. Five years in, he still wasn't feeling fulfilled. *"I had everything. I had the money. I had success. I had a great wife and a great life, but still, something was missing."* That something was the ability to help others achieve the same level of success if they wanted it. So, he embarked upon a huge experiment he calls independent capitalism.

Simbiose Ventures is a team of eleven to forty people (at any given time), mostly developers working together to develop new technologies. In the morning, they study together, and in the afternoon, they use what they learned to come up with marketable products, which they sell to generate revenue. While they are doing this, they help each other grow.

"I think the most important thing," advises Gabriel, *"is the way we think about people. You've heard it said that you hire people for their technical competencies, but you fire them due to their soft skills or lack thereof? We don't care about hard skills. We only care about soft skills."* In fact, when they go through a recruitment phase, they actively look for people who didn't come from fancy universities or have a lot of experience. Typically, they get about 300 applications every time they go through a hiring round.

They are paid based on their monthly performance in terms of soft-skills behaviors. Each position has a certain amount they are eligible to earn each month. Twenty percent of that amount is guaranteed, and 80 percent is based on how well you are rated, by your peers, in soft skills. They pair up teammates to work on projects and rate each other continuously, using specific criteria set forth by the organization. Categories include communication, teamwork, conflict and negotiation management, initiative, punctuality, and organization. Each category contains actionable and well-defined criteria that leave little room for interpretation. For instance:

Organize documents: When you create a document, you put it in the right place.

Get ahead: When you have an appointment, arrive at least two minutes before.

Inform the team: When noticing that you'll impact someone else's job, realign expectations as soon as possible.

There are almost 200 different criteria upon which team members are evaluated by their coworkers. At the end of the month, they have a sum of everything people did well and a sum of what they didn't do well. Based on that, they earn a grade of zero to 10, and where they stand reflects how much they get paid that month.

The goal is to "boost people" and help them develop their soft skills. Gabriel elaborates. *"What differentiates a great developer from a mediocre one? It's not their technical skills. It's communication. It's a willingness to learn. It's how open and vulnerable they can be to ask for help."* The "boosting," as the Simbiose team calls it, doesn't stop there. They partner people with peers based on strengths, and their job includes helping their teammates with their weaknesses. *"So, let's say I was pretty disorganized last month, and you are my peer. You're going to study something about organization, and then you're going to teach me what you learned, helping me to get more organized this month."*

They charge the team with making the system better and continuously improving their culture. Says auditor (as they call most team members at Simbiose) Giovanna Paulino, *"We have open meetings where we listen to our team members. They tell us how they think this can work better. They know each other, they know how our system works, and they know how to improve it as well. We listen to them far more often than I think other companies or teams listen to their people."* Along that same vein, Gabriel no longer considers himself the boss, preferring to work as a flattened organization, or as they say, "a team." He's the visionary and founder, but people in what might be considered "leadership" positions, go by the title Auditor, and they are committed to equal input from everyone involved.

Gabriel calls this system independent capitalism. *"Yes, there's conscious capitalism* [a more socially and ethically responsible model for business developed by John Mackey and Raj Sisodia]. *At the end of the day, conscious capitalism is a better version of capitalism, but you are not making people independent. There will still be employees, and they will continue to be employees because they will not get more money."*

Admittedly, this is an experiment. The goal is to make their team members psychically and financially independent. *"They are definitely becoming more self-aware as part of the process. When we get to the point where we are making other people more financially independent, that's when I'll be happy. We want them not to need us."* He admits he does not yet know if this is scalable, but he does know it works with a small team and believes it can work in other industries. *"It depends on how much the people at the top are willing to share."*

While this may be one of the most innovative compensation plans I've discovered yet, still in the experimental phase, it's worth noting. Rather than building the company on the backs of low-paid workers, they are committed to building their skills, confidence, and financial independence. Gabriel adds, *"I heard a presentation from a Brazilian consultant. He shared his vision for the future and, from his perspective, what it would look like. He does not believe changes will come from large revolutions, governors, or others at the top. The changes will happen in tiny groups like ours. So, maybe we're making some change here. Maybe we are starting a revolution without even knowing it. There are a lot of people who may be thinking the same way we are now, right?"*

GET FLEXIBLE WITH SCHEDULING

Certified nursing assistants (CNAs) in a skilled nursing community typically work eight-hour shifts. Seven to three, three to eleven, or eleven to seven—that is, unless you are a CNA at The Glebe in Daleville, Virginia. There, nursing assistants participate in what they call the 30/40 program. Instead of having three eight-hour shifts, they have four six-hour shifts. There are no lunch breaks, which keeps caregivers on the floor, assisting residents. CNAs work a thirty-hour work week but get paid for forty. Jonathan Cook, CEO of LifeSpire Virginia, the parent company to The Glebe, explains. *"Our basic rate of pay is $15 an hour. That's $600 a week. If you take that $600 and divide it by thirty hours, your base rate is now $20. We're paying you a ten-hour bonus."* That's also extra time to spend with your family and in your personal life.

There are rules associated with that bonus pay. *"You can't be one minute late to work, period. If you call off sick, you can switch with someone else or if there is an open shift, make it up. You're still going to get paid if you're sick, but if you don't rearrange with someone else, you miss your bonus that week."* Employees are fully eligible for benefits and paid time off, even though they aren't technically working full time.

How can they afford to pay employees more money for fewer hours? *"I can't afford not to,"* exclaims Jonathan. *"We've reduced employee turnover and have had incredible clinical outcomes."* One of the many benefits, according to their leadership, is continuity of care. Residents see the same faces every day rather than a revolving door of new caregivers. The director of nursing (DON) and the Assistant DON, who used to spend 40 percent of their day dealing with staffing issues, are now spending their time supervising, educating, supporting, and patting employees on the back. *"They're actually doing their jobs versus being firefighters."*

While you might say they are still earning the same weekly rate, they can use that extra time in ways that serve themselves. Perhaps it means fewer hours a week in daycare costs, more time with their children, or more time to work on their hobbies or side hustle. How could you get innovative with employee scheduling?

A DELICIOUS ACT OF KINDNESS AND A NEW SOURCE OF REVENUE

If you're standing in the light when you open the box, you'll notice how the cake sparkles, and you can actually see yourself in it. That's due to the shiny mirror glaze added by pastry chef Dallas Kee. The cake itself has a mascarpone mousse base, with layers of strawberry jam and an orange butter cookie, with an olive oil cake center. Or perhaps you were the recipient of the Nutella Lavender cake, with Nutella milk chocolate crunch, Lavender Cremeux, and Nutella mousse. In the center is a chocolate plate that says *Thank You!* Are you drooling yet?

Like most hotels, The Hotel at Auburn University took a hit from COVID-19. Chef Dallas was worried. *"I kept getting phone calls from my friends who were pastry chefs. 'I've been furloughed.' 'I've been laid off.' In my head, I wondered when my time was coming."* She and Hans van der Reijden began to think about what they could do for the community and came up with the idea for Acts of Kindness Cakes. *"We gave a few out to first responders and others who had done a tremendous amount in our community, with a little card that read, 'If you'd like to pay this forward, here's how you can order one,"* shares Hans. Dallas adds, *"We saw this huge number of orders come in right away. It was awesome!"* They quickly set up a website promoting the two gorgeous cakes and added special curbside desserts that you could pick up at the hotel. *"Now we have an inquiry form for wedding cakes, birthday cakes, and things of that nature."*

Not only have they generated goodwill and expressions of gratitude in the Auburn, Alabama, community, but they generated enough revenue that they could keep Chef Dallas working. Not only that but, as Dallas shares, *"I feel very empowered and grateful they trust me to do my job. I don't think I've ever had an idea they've shut down since I started in 2018. The response is always, 'Yes! Let's try it!'"*

Instead of deciding that there's no extra money to compensate your people well, why not empower them to come up with new revenue sources? You might be surprised at their creativity.

TIME TO GET CREATIVE?

I do not share these stories as recommendations for your organization. Rather, they are food for thought and examples of how others have found creative ways to compensate their people better. While certainly there are other factors that encourage employees to stay and be engaged, such as appreciation and a positive company culture, it's time to stop using those studies as an excuse for not revisiting the way you pay your people. The pay scale for low-wage workers is a conversation that's not going away. I hope you will use what you've learned in this chapter to get a little creative with your compensation.

CHAPTER EIGHT

Champion Workplace Wellness

When it comes to the wellness of their team members and the sustainability of the environment, it's all part of a larger calling for the people at ECOS. The company, which has 300 employees spread throughout four US locations and a sales team in Greece, makes safer laundry detergents and cleaning products that protect the health and wellness of people, pets, and the planet. Being a champion for wellness is all in a day's work!

"Our approach to wellness," discloses vice president of human resources Jennifer Lollino, *"is twofold. We focus on both the physical, mental, and emotional well-being of our coworkers, as well as offering them sustainability initiatives to help them be more environmentally conscious."*

The latter includes a $2,500 incentive toward the purchase of an eco-friendly automobile, whether it's a hybrid that gets at least 40 miles per highway gallon or an electric car. Employees also receive a $1,000 bonus if they move within 10 miles of the facility where they work and another $2,000 if they install solar panels on their home. *"Our employees have well received these incentives,"* reports Jennifer, *"and it kickstarts their ability to live in a more environmentally friendly way, which really fits in with our mission. We want to encourage people to reduce their carbon footprint."*

If you work for ECOS, you might also be invited to one of their twice-annual Re-Parties, the brainchild of Dr. Nadereh Afsharmanesh, the vice president of sustainability. Team members bring in gently used clothing or items they are no longer using. As the saying goes, *"One person's trash is another person's treasure. Anytime we can reuse, reduce, or re-purpose, we're making a lesser impact on the environment."*

The company is just as committed to the well-being of its employees. For instance, they worked with Dr. Daniel Amen, a psychiatrist, brain health expert, and *New York Times* bestselling author of *Your Brain Is Always Listening: Tame the Hidden Dragons that Control Your Happiness, Habits, and Hang-ups* (Tyndale Momentum, 2021). Once a month, for six months, employees attended a program called Bright Minds, which focused on improving your brain health and overall well-being.

Before the COVID-19 pandemic, employees were able to take part in weekly yoga classes. Once people began to work from home, the company offered both live virtual and on-demand courses that employees could dial into throughout the day as their schedule permitted. Pre-COVID, a chef came into the company headquarters in Cypress, California, and made healthy lunches that ECOS colleagues could purchase rather than running out to grab a fast-food meal. *"I miss them,"* says Jennifer, who at the time I write this was still mostly working from her home. In-person or virtual, the company did not waiver on its commitment to workplace wellness. They instituted Wellness Wednesday calls informing team members of a variety of topics and guest speakers. Said chef, for example, joined a call or two to provide healthy cooking classes. Once a month or so, CEO Kelly Vlahakis-Hanks conducts a town hall meeting to provide updates and dive into diversity and inclusion topics. Dr. Amen came back to talk to ECOS employees about the impact that COVID has had on everyone's emotional well-being and mental health, in addition to the physical aspect of the disease.

There is little doubt that the mental health of people globally has been severely affected over the past couple of years. We've been living through a disruption of the entire world and have sustained a series of losses—loss of life, income, and social connection. Graduations, weddings, and special events were postponed, not to mention the loss of walking down the street without being afraid of catching a disease. We're collectively grieving, and I suspect that, as a human race, we'll all be dealing with some form of post-traumatic stress going forward. Pile on political strife, racial injustice, and environmental calamities, and it's amazing any of us are holding it together. Consider how this collective grief and fear have impacted your employees. The number-one request we had at Red-Carpet Learning when we asked, *"How can we help you during these challenging times?"* was *"Help us learn how to boost employee morale! Our team is anxious and growing weary."* (Visit www.theRedCarpetWay.tv for the YouTube playlist we put together about boosting employee morale during challenging times.)

The effects on humans across the globe are real. Dentists have reported a surge in excessive teeth grinding. There have been high rates of anxiety and depression. The Recovery Village® surveyed 1,000 American adults about their use of drugs and alcohol over a month, shortly after the pandemic hit the US. Fifty-five percent of respondents reported an increase in alcohol consumption, and 18 percent reported a significant increase.[1] This list of effects from this shared trauma goes on, and truth be told, as this chapter is being written, we don't even know what the long-term impacts on physical, emotional, and financial wellness will be.

Why should you, an employer or leader, care? You want to care because as much as we liked to pretend that when you get to work, you "leave your troubles at the door," we're starting to realize that it's just not possible. You cannot separate someone's humanity from their work. *"The reality is,"* says organizational psychologist and Certified Executive Coach Krystena Sterling, *"emotions have never been left out of the workplace. Not ever. It's not possible because emotions are part of your everyday decisions. Leaders can help by being truly empathetic and honoring how emotions and our well-being fit in our lives, including our work life. Like anything, when taken to an extreme that can be negative, it's just not possible to leave your emotions at the door, so I hope everyone just quits trying."*

One study put the cost of employee stress on the workplace at $300 billion.[2] That's money out the window due to accidents, high insurance costs, absenteeism, and presenteeism, which is another way of saying your employees are present in body but not in mind.

Perhaps you should care because the workplace is often the cause of employee stress. For years we've been taught to do more with less, which, rather than mean to become more efficient as Buckminster Fuller intended when he coined the term,[3] has turned into *"let's hire fewer people and pile the work on them until they can't do anymore, and then top it with another initiative or two,"* not to mention the "essential employees" who have to work two or three jobs to feed their families because they're not getting paid a living wage. Christen Rinaldi, LCMHCA, reports,

"People come into therapy, and they talk about their work. They talk about their bosses and conflicts with coworkers. I think leadership teams are starting to recognize they need to take care of their employees; otherwise, they are going to lose good people."

It's not just the emotional and physical well-being of your employees that impact the bottom line. Denise O'Malley, a self-described reformed insurance agent who founded You Define Wellness!, shares that there are eight dimensions of wellness (defined by the Substance Abuse and Mental Health Services Administration)[4]:

1. Physical wellness includes healthy habits such as nutrition, exercise, rest, and health related to your body.
2. Emotional wellness relates to the ability to express your emotions, reduce stress, and cope with life's challenges.
3. Financial wellness incorporates a person's relationship to money. Are they in debt? Do they have savings? Can they pay their bills and manage their finances?
4. Social wellness means that people have positive human interactions. They have family and friends, and good communication, and healthy relationships with their coworkers.
5. Spiritual wellness consists of the personal values and beliefs that provide purpose for your life. It's not about practicing a particular religion or religion at all, although following a specific doctrine can be one way to spiritual wellness. Instead, it's about finding meaning in one's life and, perhaps, a connection to something larger than oneself.
6. Environmental wellness is an awareness of safety when it comes to ones' surroundings. For some, it means learning about toxins in your environment, getting out in nature, or protecting yourself from pollutants (or disease).

7. Occupational wellness relates directly to what's happening on the job. Do you feel you have a purpose? Do you have good relationships with your boss or your coworkers? Do you feel you are supported and are given the resources and education you need to do your job well?

8. Intellectual wellness consists of activities related to your learning and development, sharing your talents, and diving into pursuits that enhance your memory, focus, and critical-thinking skills.

When designing a workplace wellness program, it's key to keep all of the dimensions in mind for a well-rounded experience. Here are some other factors to keep in mind and actions to take.

BE THOUGHTFUL

Too often, organizational leaders jump into a wellness "program" for their employees as a risk-management tactic or to cut down on absenteeism without giving it much thought. They start weight-loss challenges or smoking-cessation programs that may or may not get a lot of participation. Even if people participate, the results may not be long term or move the needle in terms of business goals, so they're abandoned.

Start by talking with your people about wellness, get them thinking about their own wellness goals, and ask how you can support them. Don't make assumptions about what interests them. Ask. Denise O'Malley of You Define Wellness! relates that during a survey of employees at a construction company, more than 54 percent were interested in learning more about meditation. When we consider the stereotypical image of construction workers, meditation is not the first thing that comes to mind. Yet, more than half of their employees thought they'd find it helpful. Imagine what they would have missed out on if their team members had no input. At another organization, a questionnaire produced information that 100 percent of their employees enjoyed going camping and a significant portion of them desired to eat healthier. *"Rather than just bringing in a nutritionist,"* Denise reveals, *"we encouraged them to bring in a nutrition coach who would bring in a camp stove and teach a class on how to eat healthy in the great outdoors. When you're talking about wellness programs, you get your employees engaged by meeting them where they are and not by shoving something down their throats. Put together a wellness program that taps into the interests of your team, rather than saying, 'Hey, I heard someone did a smoothie day, so let's do that!'"*

Christen Rinaldi adds that it's important to collect and analyze data along the way. *"I don't think we take the pulse frequently enough when it comes to employees' sense of well-being and feeling heard. Get the data you need to know if you're getting ROI and if it's helping your people. It's great to hire a massage therapist, but if nobody's using the service or people don't consider it to be a benefit, then it's time to try something different."* Not to mention that the more you involve your team members in the decision-making, the more valued they will feel.

CHECK IN AND LISTEN

Once you understand that you cannot separate one's humanity from one's work life, you get how important it is to start checking in with your people. Here's an example. Diversity expert Jessica Pettitt tells the story of working with an automobile dealership:

"In the process of doing employee interviews, I learned that the Vice President of Sales and the Head Mechanic both had similar stories. They had both been considered rockstar employees, whom everyone looked up to, and all of a sudden had become incredibly lazy, leaving early, and taking long lunches.' So, here you have two people on the other side of the building, with different wardrobes, in very different pay grades, and yet both had this sudden change." Finding it interesting that these two stories could be happening simultaneously, Jess decided to investigate. It turned out that they were both going through chemotherapy at the same hospital and did not want to tell anyone because they didn't want the quality of their work to be judged. *"Talk about a self-fulfilling prophecy. I asked permission to tell their boss, who was totally taken aback, and all of a sudden, there were carpools, meal plans, and a completely new story."*

Rather than throw a wellness plan together, start by making it safe for people to talk about what's going on with them. Start the conversation and keep it going. One of the silver linings of the pandemic was that it gave people the space to say, *"Hey, I'm not doing so well. I'm afraid to get sick. My wife has lost her income. My kids are home from school, and we're struggling to get it all done."* Let's keep those conversations going. Make it safe for people to speak up and really listen, because those exchanges will help you collectively make decisions that will positively impact your people and your organization's health and wellness.

BE AWARE OF THE BURNOUT SPIRAL

In addition to being a renowned artist, Rolinda Stotts is a reboot consultant, working with individuals and companies to help them sustain beautiful, balanced lives and workplaces. Pulling from several sources, she has developed something she calls The

Burnout Spiral. She says, *"There was a magnificent American psychologist named Herbert Freudenberger, who coined the term 'burnout' in the 1970s. In my own studies, I've discovered there are actually four forms of burnout."* They are:

1. Wornout: This is when you've gone too hard, too long, too fast, and you're exhausted.
2. Rustout: This can happen when you're underestimated and/or underutilized at work. You stop learning and growing and become apathetic. Rolinda elaborates, *"Any vehicle that sits on the side of the road and doesn't get used will literally rust out and not be able to function."*
3. Whiteout: This happens when external conditions come upon us that we're not expecting, like blizzard conditions that create fear when you're driving. You're on high alert because you can't see in front of you or behind you, and it feels like danger is everywhere. Rolinda explains, *"What happens is the different forms of burnout can feed into one another. You can be in whiteout, white knuckling your way through life, which causes you to move into wornout. Your exhaustion causes apathy, which means you're in rustout. Your apathy causes problems such as losing your health, your job, or your marriage. All of that can lead to the most dangerous form of all."*
4. Blackout: Complete hopelessness, the pit of despair, and no light, leading to suicide or other forms of death.

Says Rolinda, *"When you're not aware of the warning signs, you can be spiraling and unintentionally end up in blackout."* The root cause of all forms of burnout, according to Rolinda, is an unsafe environment. Specifically, an environment with a lack of

The Burnout Spiral™

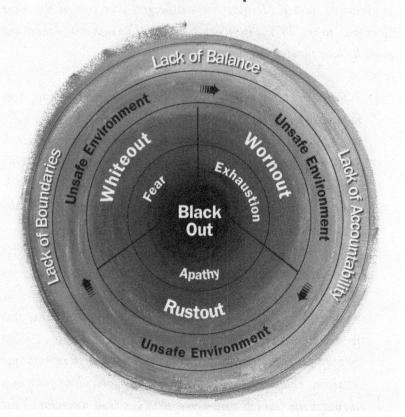

Rolinda Stotts, www.BeautifulAsIs.com

boundaries, a lack of balance, and a lack of accountability. *"The good news is that the opposite is the solution to being fully alive and living with joy, vitality, purpose, and creativity. Create an environment that has boundaries, balance, accountability."*

The first step is to pay attention. Do you see signs of burnout in your workplace? As we've already discussed, it's important to get curious and create a safe space for your people to speak up about what they're experiencing. If you notice one person on this spiral, talk to them about how you can help. If you see many people on the burnout spiral, it's time to look inward. Is it time to set boundaries with your customers and for your coworkers? Is it time to do a better job creating work-life balance for your team? Are you holding your leadership team accountable for reasonable workplace practices that promote harmony?

Furthermore, are you holding yourself accountable to boundaries and balance and leading by example? My guess is that you recognize one or more of the forms of burnout. You've probably experienced them yourself or noticed them in your employees. Now you have a language to use and actions you can take to help your team members (or yourself) get out of the spiral and into fully engaged living!

BUILD EMOTIONAL RESILIENCE

Do not underestimate the need to address mental health and emotional resilience. Consider not just the physical labor or thinking and strategizing you ask your employees to do daily, but also the emotional labor required of them. As a service culture expert, I know the value of a smile and an upbeat, friendly hello. However, Krystena Sterling reminds me, *"For some people, that's an easy ask. They like to smile and genuinely engage with others. On the flip side, if I'm not someone who likes to smile and has less of a positive outlook on life, I'm going to exert a lot of emotional labor, which is exhausting and stressful."* So, do you only hire people who have the natural gift of being positive and smile easily? Well, yes, that's one solution, although Krystena doesn't think it's realistic. *"My personal belief is that there aren't enough humans possible to only hire people that have that innate skill."*

According to Krystena, this is where emotional intelligence (EQ) comes in. The four quadrants of emotional intelligence are self-awareness, self-management, understanding others, and understanding the environment around you. *"When it comes to emotional labor, it's about understanding your emotions, understanding others, and being able to regulate your emotions. The higher the degree of emotional intelligence a person has, the easier it is to, for instance, mimic a behavior like a smile without expending a ton of energy and still being totally authentic,"* says Krystena. Consider how educating your team members about emotional intelligence can assist them in situations such as facing an upset or irate customer. In fact, the first step in that situation is for the person on the receiving end to regulate their own emotions to focus on the customer and do their best to help without taking the situation personally. According to Krystena, one of the best first steps is for leaders to know their own EQ level and understand what tools are available to help themselves and their employees. Don't stop at leadership, though! Invest in helping your employees identify and navigate their own emotions, and you'll build resiliency and intentionality within your team.

ADOPT MORE SUPPORTIVE PRACTICES AND POLICIES

Is it time to look at how you might be contributing to the stress your employees are feeling? Start by looking at everything you ask them to do. How many of your team members take work home because they can't get it done on the job? How many have complained about your piling on initiative after initiative (which often end up being the flavor of that year), only to have you ignore their pleas? Wouldn't it be better to do a few things well than encourage your team to do more, more, more with less?

It's time for leaders to *"take humanity into account and not have it negatively impact a person on a professional level. Work to make it sustainable that people can have real work-life balance,"* says mental health counselor Christen Rinaldi. This might be working in benefits like flextime, mental health days, daycare vouchers, an onsite daycare facility, or pumping rooms for breastfeeding mothers. She reports, *"Prior to having my own practice, I worked at a company where I was allowed to have my baby on my hip for the first six months. I was able to sit there at my computer and breastfeed because it was a really family-friendly workplace. It enabled me to get my work done successfully and be there for my child."* Consider that as a result of the COVID-19 pandemic, women were forced out of the workforce at disproportionately high rates, according to the National Bureau of Economic Research.[5] This is partly due to the closure or negative impact on industries that attract more female employees, such as hair salons, personal care services, and food preparation. Another is that, with children taken out of the traditional school environment, most childcare and education responsibilities fell on women.

Employers can help their team members achieve better balance between their work life and home life by:

- Encouraging people to take breaks and vacation.
- Extending vacations or even offering unpaid vacations.
- Offering the choice of working remotely whenever possible.
- Focusing more on productivity than on "hours worked."
- Regularly reviewing the workloads of your employees and making changes when they are out of balance.

- Ending intrusive practices like emailing your team members at night or on weekends and expecting their reply.
- Setting boundaries with customers and providing realistic expectations.
- Leading by example by being rigorous with your own wellness practices.

There will, of course, always be times when that balance is out of whack. The key is to ensure those heavy commitment times are few and far between and not par for the course. As a leader, you can help by noticing when your team members are putting in that extra effort. One of my favorite bosses pulled me aside after a successful event that I had spent weeks planning and executing and surprised me by saying, *"Take tomorrow off and enjoy your long weekend. You've earned it."* That's the kind of moment that makes you feel valued and that the extra time you put in was all worth it! That's the kind of boss you'd do anything for!

EDUCATE AND OFFER RESOURCES

Lucy Henry is the vice president of stakeholder relations for First Sun EAP Alliance, Inc., based in Columbia, South Carolina. She points out, *"You might notice that coworkers aren't getting along, there's absenteeism, people are working but 'just aren't there,' or there's poor performance and increased mistakes. What's happening in the workplace may be just the tip of the iceberg. What's underneath that iceberg are financial problems, legal problems, family problems, substance abuse problems, a medical diagnosis, or caregiving for an elderly parent. You can help get people back on track at work by providing resources to those employees and their family* members so they can get the assistance they need." Many organizations have Employee Assistance Programs (EAPs) as part of their benefits package, but do your employees even know about them? Used effectively, EAPs can be excellent resources for the well-being of your people.

Again, one of the positive effects of the pandemic is that it gave people permission to speak up and say, *"Hey! I need help."* Several of our Red-Carpet Learning clients offered their team members meditation rooms to take fifteen-minute breaks, offered hazard pay to help financially, and even set up food pantries to help employees feed their families. Needing help was destigmatized in a way. I hope this continues, because there isn't a single person in the world who doesn't need assistance sometimes.

So, if you have an EAP, perhaps you could do a better job of promoting it. Lucy warns, *"Know that not every Employee Assistance Program is equal. If you have one that's not meeting your needs, then find one that will."*

There are other ways you can offer support as well. With You Define Wellness!, for example, Denise O'Malley has created a network of hundreds of health and wellness professionals across the United States. She offers employer-subsidized care for more than 130 modalities in that network. *"It's everything from acupuncture to zone balancing, and everything in between focused on the eight dimensions of wellness. We are not a replacement for medical insurance but rather a sampler platter, introducing people to healing modalities they've perhaps never experienced before."*

If you've checked in with your team and really listened, then you may have a good sense of what's needed at any given time. Perhaps you can offer a financial coach to help your people budget and save and empower them around money. You might consider putting an employee concierge on staff to help people with their dry cleaning, auto repair, childcare arrangements, or dinner reservations. Employees pay for the cost of each service, but the employer pays for the concierge. If it's physical wellness, it might be an onsite gym, or it might be encouragement to walk more. Years ago, for instance, I read about a hospital that decorated the stairwells with brightly colored paint and motivational signs, piped in energizing music, and even added encouraging phrases on each step to motivate their healthcare workers to take the stairs instead of the elevator.

There are many resources you can provide to assist your team members with their specific wellness needs. The keys are to listen to your team, be thoughtful about the process, be creative with your approach, and encourage people to take advantage of what you have to offer.

JUST SAY NO TO ADULTITIS®

According to artist, author, and professional speaker Jason Kotecki, Adultitis® is a condition that happens to us often when we lose our childlike spirit and our sense of possibility, curiosity, creativity, and joyfulness. In short, the swelling of the adult can lead to a dull, gray, joyless life. Does that mean the key to workplace wellness is bringing Play-Doh to your meetings or installing a foosball table? Not necessarily. *"It's about being human and taking your work seriously without taking yourself too seriously,"* elaborates Jason, the co-founder of Escape Adulthood. *"Here's an example. I got a chance to speak at a Technical College in Wisconsin, and the Dean was showing me around their newly renovated offices. There was cubicle space with a little plate attached that said 'The*

Awesome Room!' The Dean told me that they asked employees to give input on naming different spaces as the offices were being renovated, and this became The Awesome Room! It didn't look awesome, it was a pretty average cubicle, but I thought of all the staff meetings where someone might say, 'Hey, Bill and Susan, would you go into The Awesome Room and come up with a really great idea on this topic?'"

Jason also noticed a bulletin board with posted photos of people dressed alike. *"'Oh, that's our twins board,' explained the Dean. 'Anytime someone comes into work dressed similarly to someone else—say two people wear purple that day—we take a picture and put it on the twins board.'"*

"What struck me about that," says Jason, *"isn't that if you change the name of your rooms, your culture will get better, but rather that the vibe of this team was really cohesive, and it felt like they were all so happy to be there."* It's not about the specific ways you bring fun into the workplace, but rather having empathy for the people you work with and allowing them to be their most joyful, authentic selves while on the job. Create a culture where that's allowed, and people will bring their own fun. Says Jason, *"The part that merriment plays in wellness is something a lot of people miss out on because they are afraid that if they let their people have fun, they will not do their work. That's a pretty low bar to set for your people."* Agreed. My experience is that people will rise to the level you expect of them.

Whether it's the dental offices that buy the fabulous Escape Adulthood calendar every year and incorporate the special holidays, like cupcake day, into their monthly celebrations or the banker who has a beautiful landscape painting on his wall with a tiny little Winnie the Pooh and Piglet sitting at the edge of it, or the Madison, Wisconsin, designer company that hosts a monthly employee spoons tournament, there are a variety of different tools you can use to spark workplace whimsy! *"However,"* warns Jason, *"if there are no roots, it won't stick."*

IT'S NOT FLUFF. IT'S YOUR CULTURE.

Are you starting to see that there isn't a magic wand approach that will fix your employee engagement and retention issues? It's about your culture.

This chapter started with a story about ECOS, and you can see precisely how their wellness efforts fit into their mission. However, you don't have to be focused on environmentally friendly products to understand how the eight aspects of wellness impact your people and your organizational culture. Stop thinking about it as fluff, destigmatize the need to address mental health, and start having real conversations about how you can support your team and coworkers to be the best versions of themselves both in and out of the workplace.

CHAPTER NINE

Create a Safe Space

As far as workplace safety goes, Hans van der Reijden, founder and CEO of Ithaka Hospitality Partners, knows who has all the answers: your team members, of course. The hospitality group manages, among other properties, The Hotel at Auburn University in eastern Alabama. In 2020, immediately after the pandemic took hold, occupancy dropped to a record low of 7 percent, slowly climbing to 12, 15, and 20 percent, and was at about 40 percent when I spoke to Hans in January 2021. Keep in mind, this is without the typical number of meetings and conventions hosted by the hotel and convention center on an annual basis. Guest reviews that year were extremely positive, with 93 percent of their guests rating their stay a 9 or 10 on a 10-point scale. One review on Trip Advisor, which the reviewer entitled "The Way to Run a Hotel In a Pandemic," wrote, ". . . *Manager Paul Reggio and his entire team should teach classes on how to serve its guests while maintaining all needed safety and healthy protocol. They find creative ways to say 'yes' where it seems that many other hotels too easily say 'no.'"*

Interesting, considering that Hans told his team from the very beginning, *"Don't come to me with excuses about why we should stop doing something. Instead, tell me how we're going to do it responsibly and safely."*

The first step was staying ahead of the guidelines of the CDC, the American Hotel and Lodging Association, and the National Restaurant Association. The hotel had installed plexiglass barriers earlier than most *("before the prices tripled,"* confides Hans), and *"our front desk manager figured out how guests could do touchless check-in before the end of March."* The hotel participated in a beta certification program by Forbes Travel Guide and Sharecare. com to verify their health and safety standards in the era of COVID-19. *"We worked with them for months, and the certifying bodies observed us to see that we were actually following the processes we promoted."* This impressed me because, as someone who traveled with her husband and dogs from Asheville, North Carolina, to St. Paul, Minnesota, to visit her mother-in-law, I can tell you that the promises made by many hotels were not being followed consistently. Let's just say that I saw enough unmasked housekeepers breathing over the bedsheets to be thankful that Jim and I brought our own linens. Hans agrees. *"When you walk into a hotel, and you watch their impressive video, but then spy employees walking around without masks or handling food in an unsanitary way, that's false advertising. The key is your culture. Have you selected intentionally and nurtured people, so they are driven to create experiences for guests and coworkers because they feel joy when they do?"*

The Hotel at Auburn University was one of the first twenty-nine hotels worldwide to become Sharecare Health Security VERIFIED® with Forbes Travel Guide, and the only non-five-star property on the list! Says Hans, *"It was a great boost for our team members to experience this. They thought, 'WOW, this is what we're doing to keep ourselves, our coworkers, and our guests safe!'"* This sense of pride led to team members coming to the leadership team with more ideas. *"The mantra of 'Don't come to me with excuses about why we should stop doing something but tell me how we're going to be able to continue to do it in a safe and responsible way' changed the perspective within the team inside the hotel."* They held brainstorming sessions and came up with revenue-generating ideas and best practices to keep up the traditions coworkers and guests had come to love. As a result, they could retain all but eight employees after their PPP monies had run out. They safely threw a socially distanced farewell reception for their culinary interns from the Philippines and South Korea, who shared that their peers working elsewhere were simply told "Your internship is over. Please find your way home." Opening day for the Auburn Tigers is typically a huge day in the hotel. Two bartenders who've been with the company for thirty-two years were within the generation hit hardest by COVID-19. However, inspired by the hotel's safety precautions, they showed up, as usual, decked out in orange and blue, wearing masks, staying behind the plexiglass, and getting assistance from younger coworkers to collect payment. Hans recalls, *"It was hilarious, and the bartenders, coworkers, and guests alike had a ball!"* The hotel is famous for its annual massive gingerbread village held over the holidays. Working with the building science program on campus, the students build 3D models out of wood, and the hotel staff covers them with gingerbread. Each department adopts one of the twenty-two buildings and decorates a gingerbread house. Coworkers would squeeze into a meeting room with candy, cookies, and Christmas music and have a blast decorating their submissions. Inspired by the mantra of *"Tell me how we're going to do it safely,"* someone came forward with the idea of hosting it in their empty convention center. There was candy, cookies, and Christmas music, but it was safe, sanitized, and socially distanced. The event typically draws about 2,500 people after the town holiday parade, but Hans thought, *"With Covid, we're lucky if we get 200."* They added line extensions, physically distanced "footprints" to guide guests, and required and provided masks, and *"We ended up with 1,000 people!"* The hotel employees gained a great sense of pride! *"Again, it goes back to not stopping something, but rather finding a way to do it safely and responsibly, and the best part was that our team members were driving it."*

Like most things, when it comes to your employees and your customers' safety, one of the best practices you can engage in is to involve your team. Hans exclaims, *"It's almost like everyone locked arms and said, 'We're going to push through and march forward. We're going to do this, even with six feet in between!'"*

The Hotel at Auburn University provides a beautiful example of creating a safe environment in terms of the pandemic while carrying on successfully. Keeping your employees and customers safe from disease and accidents is indeed a high priority. However, there are also other aspects of creating a safe work environment. For instance, it's imperative to make it safe for your employees to share ideas, make mistakes, or safe from bullying or harassment. Sometimes creating a safe workspace means setting boundaries with your customers or creating a safety net with like-minded people. Let's explore those aspects.

SAFE TO SHARE IDEAS

Amy Edmondson, the Harvard University professor who coined the term *psychological safety,* defines it as a belief that one will not be punished or humiliated for speaking up with ideas, questions, concerns, or mistakes.[1] If you notice people in your organization timid to contribute their opinions, your workplace may not be as safe as you think it is. *"We're no different in the boardroom* [or the workplace] *than we were back on the playground or in middle school. We fear judgment. We fear ridicule. We fear being wrong,"* reminds Mike Domitrz from the Center for Respect. However, until leaders draw a line in the sand and set the example that ridiculing, belittling, and dismissing your coworkers is unacceptable, you're going to have employees working in psychologically unsafe environments. So, what do you do to create an atmosphere of mutual respect among teammates? First, work with your employees to define ground rules for how you will work together.

Then, be prepared to intervene when the opposite happens. *"Intervening,"* says Mike, *"is ultimately a key element to create a culture of respect because people are going to be thoughtless at times, and if you don't have a way to intercede, the disrespect will build and build."* So, what does that mean? *"I was speaking to an audience full of CEOs and a President of an organization raises his hand. He says, 'There's a woman on our board of directors, and we have this one guy who just runs over her words and belittles and dismisses her. What should I do?' Well, imagine if at that moment you interrupted and said, 'John, please let Susie finish. We'd love to hear her complete thought.' This tells Susie and everyone else in the room that she matters. Then, you go back to John, and he knows that his voice matters too."* Mike suggests that as a leader, you go into each situation intending to stand for everyone in the room. This means that you are present to what everyone wants to share and may not be sharing. It may mean that you ask the quietest person what their thoughts are or, if you sense they are uncomfortable, ask them to consider your question and come back in a day or two with their ideas. It also means to encourage everyone to allow each person to contribute and finish their thoughts while at the same time not diminishing the person interrupting. *"You don't respond to disrespect with more disrespect."*

Mike and I agree that creating a safe space for people to share and collaborate starts by educating people at the highest levels of the organization and going deeper and deeper because, as leaders, everything you do sets the foundation for your culture.

SAFE TO MAKE MISTAKES

I once heard a colleague say that anytime one of his team members made a big mistake, he gave them $100 because he considered it a great learning experience. While you may not want to go that far, it is to your benefit to make it safe for your employees to fail. The reason the phrases *It's not my job* and *I don't know* are so prevalent in the workplace is that people are afraid if they do or say the wrong thing, they'll receive the metaphorical hand slap.

At one company where the Red-Carpet team had rolled out our "Treat Your Customers Like STARS" curriculum, people became excited to run out and surprise and delight their customers. In doing so, the challenge was that they occasionally forgot about some of the procedural basics their managers thought were important. A manager told me about one such incident and said that, when she questioned the employee, he said, *"I was trying to personalize the experience for (the customer), and he was thrilled."* She replied, *"Well, that's all well and good, but you can't leave your station to do it. Jeez!"* How often do you think that team member went out on a limb to create an extraordinary customer experience after that? Probably not often. One way you make it safe for people to make mistakes is to celebrate their initiative first, and then coach them to accomplish the same goal but safely and responsibly.

It's also helpful to own up to your own errors. Christen Rinaldi suggests, *"One book that should be on every leader's shelf (and on their minds and hearts) is Harriet Lerner's* Why Won't You Apologize? Healing Big Betrayals and Everyday Hurts [Gallery Books, January 2017]." Leaders are sometimes afraid that if they apologize, they'll seem weak. On the contrary, you'll seem human, and if you can use your mistakes to demonstrate what you've learned, then your team will feel free-er to step up and out to try something new and see mistakes as excellent learning opportunities.

SAFE FROM BULLYING AND HARASSMENT

Remember your neighborhood bully? Our neighborhood had two. Butchy and Jeffrey. Just typing their names sends shivers up my spine. I had to pass their house every morning as I walked to the bus stop, and I would pray they wouldn't be outside because, if they were, I would surely be the subject of hurtful comments, taunts, and even threats. Once, along with two other boys, they formed a circle around me and wouldn't let me move past for several minutes while I stood there crying in fear. The sad truth is that bullying is not only a childhood affliction. It happens in the workplace more than you might imagine. A 2019 study by Monster.com of more than 2,000 employees found that 90 percent stated they had been bullied in the workplace, 51 percent said a boss bullied them, 39 percent said a coworker bullied them, and 4 percent said the perpetrator was a customer.[2] Bullying can look like any of these behaviors:[3]

- Threats, degradation and humiliation, or verbal abuse
- Gossip
- Mean-spirited pranks
- Angry, aggressive, and condescending language
- Repeatedly picking apart someone's work
- Withholding necessary information or sabotaging someone's work
- Social isolation and exclusion

Karen Maher, a former lawyer turned work health and safety culture consultant, who currently works with companies in Australia, tells me that they didn't even have a definition in the country until recently. Says Karen, *"It's repeated and unreasonable behavior directed towards a worker or group of workers that creates a risk to health and safety."* She firmly believes that in addition to being a humankind issue, it is a risk management issue. *"We've had a big shift in Australia in terms of focusing on workplace bullying and harassment because it's been a huge issue. We had several cases in the early 2000s where people took their own lives as a result of workplace bullying."* Surely, it's a risk and a reality globally, with suicide, now being the 10th-leading cause of death with rates rising in record numbers.[4] When bullying is allowed to continue in your company, employees can suffer from anxiety, depression, panic attacks, and sleep disorders, among a host of other problems. Maher suggests taking a proactive approach to prevent it from happening in the first place. *"First, ask the right questions during your recruitment process so you can weed out people who aren't going to fit with your values. Secondly, get clear with your managers and team members about what behavior is okay and not okay. When you see it happening, get on top of it quickly and nip it in the bud. You know the saying—what you're willing to look past is a standard you accept."*

To help organizations create a culture where bullying isn't tolerated, Karen has developed her SMART® Culture Solution.

S = Safety Focus (Your workplace isn't safe if bullying is allowed.)

M = Measurable (You've got to measure the impact of your training and hold people accountable.)

A = Awareness (It's important to shine a light on the issue.)

R = Respect (Underneath an anti-bullying policy lies the foundation of respect.)

T = Team (It's up to everyone on the team to be committed to a respectful workplace.)

Then there's keeping people safe from sexual harassment.

When Stephanie Angelo was in her late twenties, she worked for a married couple as an office administrator. She was often alone with her male boss when his wife was out of the office. During those times, he would do things like stand behind her if she was balancing the checkbook, or point to something and use it as an excuse to rub his hand up her breast. *"I'd be sitting there frozen, wondering. Should I ignore him? Should I say something? Not knowing what to do,"* recalls Stephanie.

About that same time, she was awoken during the night by a male neighbor who broke into her apartment and attempted to rape her. She fought him off and, when he left, she called the police. Naturally, she was nervous about staying at her apartment, so when her bosses offered to let her stay in their guest bedroom, she gratefully accepted. *"However, they would invite friends over for barbeques, and I would catch him and a friend climbing up to look in on me in the guest bedroom and bathroom. I was humiliated, so I would barricade myself in the closet or somewhere there was no window. I never told his wife, and I was single, alone, and needed the job."*

Today Stephanie Angelo is a consultant and speaker on the topic of company culture, and has twenty years of experience in human resources. *"The employer has to care,"* she advises. *"In my case, I didn't feel like I had anyone to talk to. Women are put into a position where they need the job, and no one is going to hear their voice."*

Rena Romano survived incest at the hands of her older brother when she was four years old. When she was in her twenties, she worked at a landscaping firm. She was the only woman working with several men. The company owner would massage her back, make sexual overtones, and try to get her to engage in inappropriate acts with him. In addition, a colleague who worked out in the field would tease her, belittle her, and make threats that he was going to break into her home and get her. Says Rena, *"Just as I was starting this job, a friend of mine was raped. She went to the police, and they blamed her for enticing the violent act. As a result, I felt like there was no one I could tell about my own situation."*

One night, her coworker did break into her home while she was asleep in her bed, pinned her down, and raped her. *"When he slithered out of the house, I took a shower. I knew I couldn't go to the police, and I couldn't tell my boss the next day because he was sexually harassing me."* Rena found another job shortly after that.

Today Rena is an author, activist, and speaker who has shared her story both on *The Oprah Winfrey Show* and on the TEDx stage advises, *"It's important that people listen to the victim, without interruption, and without judgment."* She recommends what she calls the "praise approach." Rather than questioning someone who comes forward, you first praise them for their bravery in doing so. She tells her story because, she says, *"I grew tired of being ashamed of a crime I did not commit."*

These stories happened many years ago, and thanks to Anita Hill and others, laws have changed. Don't kid yourself, though: It still happens, and it is still true in many cases that the victims are blamed or, at the very least, questioned.

I have my own stories. When I was a hostess in a restaurant, the owner's brother used to hang out at the hostess stand and talk to me about my breasts. There was the husband of an employer who hit on me repeatedly. Still, when the #MeToo movement happened, and so many of my friends began to tell their stories, I was shocked at how prevalent this kind of behavior has been. Harassment. Groping. Rape. While you may not be a perpetrator, it's essential to know what you, as a leader, can do to change a culture that allows this type of abuse to happen. Mike Domitrz states the critical language for leaders to learn is *"If anybody has harmed you psychologically, physically, or in any way, I am here for you."* It does not invite people to come forward if you say they will be punished or you threaten to harm the perpetrator. *"Tell me that you're going to be there for me and that you're going to help me move forward."* Then, of course, listen, investigate, and stand by your decision to create a safe space for your people. Says Mike, *"If you make a statement like 'I'm here for you,' but then you do or say something incongruent, then you haven't created a safe space. A leader who cares about this will come from a human level and dig deeper to discover what it means to create a safe environment. If you are a CEO who focuses on avoiding lawsuits over creating safe spaces, the people you lead will learn how not to get caught instead of doing the right thing. That 'cover your butt' approach results in a highly toxic and dangerous culture. If you are a CEO focused on creating a SAFE Space, everyone stands for each other and works to build a culture of respect (and of course, then lawsuits are dramatically less likely to ever happen)."*

SAFE FROM YOUR CUSTOMERS

Sometimes it's a customer, not a coworker, that's behaving badly. Paige Arnof-Fenn is the founder of a global branding and digital marketing firm called Mavens & Moguls. She recalls one such customer:

> "We had one client on a $10,000 a month retainer for a one-year agreement, so this was a six-figure engagement. This would be exciting, except that the guy treated us so poorly. We got him into the *New York Times, Wall Street Journal,* and *Washington Post,* all the big media, but all he did was complain at every meeting. On top of that, we had to chase him down for payment. One of my biggest fears is that we would start attracting nasty customers because they would think, 'Well if they can get all this press for that jerk, imagine what they could do for me!' This was not the kind of clientele I was looking for. So, about three months into the contract, I fired him as a client at a meeting that included three of my team members. My

team couldn't believe it, and they were thrilled! They un-derstood that I had their backs. I've got a no-jerks policy internally and a no-jerks policy externally. We freed up so much energy leaving behind that negativity that within weeks we had replaced the revenue and then some, with much better clients."

Sometimes it's the customer that has to go! Did the Red-Carpet Customer Service queen really just say that? You bet your bottom dollar I did. If you keep people on who repeatedly treat your team like dirt, the message you send to your employees is "You don't matter," and that's no way to inspire them to roll out the red carpet for your more respectful customers.

IT'S ABOUT CULTURE, NOT CHECKBOXES

Yes, everything we've talked about in this chapter can be about mitigating risk in your workplace. However, if that's the reason you're taking action, then it isn't about creating a better employee experience, is it? What many companies do, for instance, is roll out a one-time anti-bullying or harassment training and then "check off that box," as though their approach made a difference.

This is about your culture. Have you built trust with your team members? Do they know you have their back and that you genuinely care about them? Hans van der Reijden walks The Hotel at Auburn University's hallways and engages with his team. *"It's about connecting and building relationships with them. You want to build a relationship that is strong enough that they are willing to share and then, in turn, decide what you can do to support them,"* says Hans.

CHAPTER TEN

Keep Your Remote Team Connected

Irina Papuc and Zach Boyette may be two of the coolest people on the planet. At least, that's what I thought to myself after our first conversation. They are the co-founders and managing partners of Galactic Fed™, which their website describes as a fully distributed company of growth marketing nerds. They have about 100 team members, in twelve different countries, who work entirely in a remote fashion and have since the company's inception in 2017. During our conversation, when the ability to travel was limited due to the pandemic, Irina was logging on from her hometown of Chicago, Illinois, and Zach was staying with family in Tennessee. At any other time, they might have been working from Latin America, Asia, or somewhere in Africa. Zach hasn't paid rent since 2016, preferring instead to live as a full-time nomad. *"Fun factoid,"* reveals Irina. *"Throughout my entire career, I've never worked in an office."* They have no corporate headquarters, and they are located somewhere on the planet at any given time. Team members have traveled to more than sixty-eight countries while working at Galactic Fed. As someone

- It's important that employees feel valued. A hand-written thank-you note goes a long way.
- If a team member does something great, recognize them immediately! Don't wait for monthly communication. Words of appreciation, big or small, can do so much to make them feel valued.

You could also utilize email, a printed newsletter, or even a monthly podcast that could be listened to in the car to provide company-wide updates, read positive reviews from clients, and give team members appreciation shout-outs. Utilize contests or other fun tactics to encourage your road warriors to tune in while they drive from client to client.

Let's wrap this chapter up with a quote that Irina brought to my attention by Arthur C. Clarke, the British science-fiction author of *2001: A Space Odyssey*. Here's an excerpt within which he predicts, in 1964, the future of remote work:

> It will be possible in that age, perhaps only fifty years from now, for (mankind) to conduct (their) business from Tahiti or Bali just as well as (they) could from London. In fact, if it proves worthwhile, almost any executive skill, administrative skill, even many physical skills could be made independent of distance . . . Men (and women) will no longer commute, they will communicate. They won't have to travel for business anymore, they'll only travel for pleasure.[3]

What's Next?

You have a choice. You can go back to how you were doing things before and keep tap dancing around the same issues, not getting the results you desire. Or, you can choose to go deep and have the provocative conversations that lead to real change.

If you choose the latter, put your employees first! Go to them with an open heart and an open mind and ask, *"What can we do to make the experience of working here a better one?"* Listen intently to their answers and partner together to picture a place that fills people with a sense of purpose—a place where empathy, curiosity, and respect prevail. Imagine if everyone could show up 100 percent as their authentic selves without fear or anxiety. Envision what it would be like to feel safe, and well, and appreciated. Consider what it means to be *connected*.

Get together as a team and use the stories, examples, and ideas in this book to inspire you as you reimagine and reinvent your employee experience. Work with each other to explore the following questions:

1. How do our people make a difference in the lives of others? How can we keep that focus in the forefront?

2. What truly makes people feel valued, and how can we prioritize authentic appreciation in our organization?

3. How can we roll out the red carpet for people from day one?

4. What does it mean to get curious about each other, and what is our language of empathy and respect?

5. How can we build a more diverse, equitable, and inclusive workplace? How can we show kindness and care for one another, even when we disagree?

6. How can we be more intentional about our communication with one another?

7. How can we create a safe space for everyone?

8. What does wellness look like in our workplace?

9. How can we be more connected a year from now than we are right now?

10. What would it take to compensate each individual who works here so they can easily take care of themselves and their families?

11. How do we get more creative with compensation?

12. What are we doing well right now? Where is there room for improvement? What are we going to do going forward to become better employers, leaders, and colleagues?

Five minutes ago, as I was in the middle of writing this wrap-up, I got a call from the CEO of a healthcare organization. We discussed many topics, but he said something that I've heard from so many people over the last twelve months: *"This year has been so very hard on my team and me. The toughest year in my entire career."*

You and I are in the middle of an incredible worldwide transformation. People everywhere are feeling the grief and pain that come with unprecedented change and uncertainty. We've felt powerless at the hands of world leaders, experts, and decision-makers. It's time we take our power back. You see, lasting change doesn't happen at the global level or even at the national level. It occurs at the local level, and that means it begins with you and me. We make the change by deciding how we're going to treat each person we encounter, be they the people we work with, the customers we serve, our family and friends, or strangers on the street. You have a choice to take your ordinary interactions and turn them into meaningful encounters by treating that person in front of you with dignity, respect, care, and love. As a leader, you have an outstanding opportunity to lift people up and out of their pain by shining a light on the good you see in them. You can stand for and with people and see in them what they may not see in themselves. When you take *that* responsibility as seriously as you do the numbers and the spreadsheets, you're not just creating a place where people want to work, you're creating a world where people want to live.

Sound lofty? Maybe, but I don't think it is. Nor do I think you sacrifice profits when you focus on people. When you prioritize people, include them, develop, mentor, and inspire them, elevate, protect, and pay them, there is no limit to what you can achieve together.

Choose to lead with your heart and see what happens. Are you ready? Let's go!

CHAPTER NOTES

INTRODUCTION

1. Heskett, James L., Thomas O. Jones, Gary W. Loveman, W. Earl Sasser, Jr., and Leonard A. Schlesinger. "Putting the Service Profit Chain to Work." *Harvard Business Review*, July–April 2008.
2. "HR Sentiment Study." 2020. *FutureWorkplace.com*.
3. "2019 Retention Report." Work Institute. *www.workinstitute.com*

CHAPTER ONE

1. Deloitte. "The Deloitte Global Millennial Survey." January 14, 2020. *www2.deloitte.com*.
2. "How Millennials Want to Work and Live." Gallup, 2016. *www.gallup.com*.
3. "Employee Retention Report: The Real Story Why Your Employees Are Leaving for Good." TINYpulse, 2018. *www.tinypulse.com*.
4. Harter, Jim. "Employee Engagement Continues Historic Rise amid Coronavirus." *Gallup.com*, May 29, 2020.

CHAPTER TWO

1. Des Georges, Colette. "Can Employee Recognition Help You Keep Them Longer?" *www.surveymonkey.com*.
2. Nelson, Dr. Bob. *1,001 Ways to Engage Employees: Help People Do Better What They Do Best* (Career Press, 2018).

CHAPTER THREE

1. "The Impact and Statistics of Civility and Incivility." Walk the Ridge. *walktheridge.com.*
2. Various reviews. Indeed.com. *www.indeed.com.*
3. Brown, Brene. "Brene Brown on Empathy." YouTube, uploaded by RSA. December 10, 2013.
4. "2020 State of Workplace Empathy." Business Solver. *www .businessolver.com.*
5. Islamic Network Groups (ING) staff. "First Principles of Religion: Treat Others as You Would Like to Be Treated (The Golden Rule)." *ING.org.*

CHAPTER FOUR

1. "Onboarding Best Practices: The Four C's." *HRCloud.com,* November 13, 2020.
2. Mann, Annamarie. "Why We Need Best Friends at Work." Gallup Workplace, January 15, 2018.
3. Reilly, Kate. "5 Insights from LinkedIn's Last Research on what Candidates Want." July 24, 2017. *www.linkedin.com.*

CHAPTER FIVE

1. "About." *Buffer.com.*
2. Griffis, Hailley. "We've Never Calculated How Long People Stay at Our Company Until Now—Here's What We Learned." *Buffer.com,* October 26, 2017.
3. Chestnut, Eleanor, and Ellen Markman. "'Girls Are as Good as Boys at Math' Implies That Boys are Probably Better: A Study of Expressions of Gender Equality." *Cognitive Science,* 42.10.1111/ cogs.12637, 2018.
4. Musser, Chris, and Gerard Taboada. "Use Internal Communications to Execute a Winning Strategy." Gallup Workplace, July 9, 2020.

5. Jouny, Valene. "10 Shocking Internal Communication Stats You Can't Ignore." *smarp.com*, June 4, 2020.

6. Ward, Toby. "The Social Intranet Report." Precient Digital Media, Version 2, February 2012. *www.prescientdigital.com*.

7. Porath, Christine. "Half of Employees Don't Feel Respected by their Bosses." *Harvard Business Review*, November 19, 2014.

8. Gascoigne, Joel. "Reflecting on 10 Years of Building Buffer." *Buffer.com*, November 30, 2020. *buffer.com*.

9. Burkus, David. "Work Friends Make Us More Productive (Except When They Stress Us Out)." *Harvard Business Review*, May 26, 2017.

CHAPTER SIX

1. Ricketts, Mark. "The Pandemic of Racism—Message from Mark Ricketts, President & CEO." June 10, 2020. *www .nationalchurchresidences.org*.

2. Nix, Elizabeth. "Tuskegee Experiment: The Infamous Syphilis Study." *History.com*, updated December 15, 2020.

3. "It's Torture Not Therapy: A Global Overview of Conversion Therapy—Practices, Perpetrators, and the Role of States." *Irct. org*, 2020.

4. Partin, Ken. "A Letter from Ken Partin, CEO, on Social Inequality." June 5, 2020. *www.givenshighlandfarms.org*.

5. Lorenzo, Rocio, and Martin Reeves. "How and Where Diversity Drives Financial Performance." *Harvard Business Review*, January 30, 2018.

6. DeHaas, Deborah L., Brent Bachus, and Eliza Horn. "Unleashing the Power of Inclusion." Deloitte University. *www2.deloitte.com*.

7. *www.MikeWileyProductions.com*.

8. Derek DelGaudio's *In & of Itself*. Directed by Frank Oz. Hulu, 2020.

9. Pettitt, Jessica. "How to Matter—Good Enough Now." *youtube.com*. Uploaded by Jess Pettitt, August 27, 2015.

CHAPTER SEVEN

1. "What Is the Living Wage?" Ontario Living Wage Network. *www.ontariolivingwage.ca.*
2. Shetty, Aastha. "Waterloo Region's Living Wage Is $16.35 Per Hour." *KitchenerToday.com*, November 2019.
3. Morad, Renee. "It's 2021 and Women STILL Make 82 Cents for Every Dollar Earned by a Man." *NBCnews.com*, March 23, 2021.

CHAPTER EIGHT

1. LaNeve, Nicole (editor). "Survey Shows Drug and Alcohol Use on the Rise During the Pandemic." December 17, 2020. *www.therecoveryvillage.com.*
2. "Financial Costs of Job Stress," UMASS Lowell. *www.uml.edu.*
3. "About Fuller." Buckminster Fuller Institute website. *www.bfi.org.*
4. "Creating a Healthier Life: A Step by Step Guide to Wellness. SAMHSA. *store.samhsa.gov.*
5. Washington, Kemberly. "COVID-19 Is Forcing Women from the Workplace in Record Numbers and We Don't Know When They'll Be Back." *Forbes.com*, October 19, 2020.

CHAPTER NINE

1. Detert, James R., and Amy C. Edmondson. "Why Employees Are Afraid to Speak." *Harvard Business Review,* May 2007.
2. Bortz, Daniel. "What Can I Do about Workplace Bullying?" *www.monster.com.*
3. "How to Identify and Manage Workplace Bullying." *Healthline.com.*
4. "Suicide Prevention: Fast Facts." Centers for Disease Control and Prevention website. *www.cdc.gov.*

CHAPTER TEN

1. "The 2021 State of Remote Work Report." *Buffer.com.*
2. "News Releases." Global Workplace Analytics. *globalwork placeanalytics.com.*
3. InfowarsMontreal, "Arthur C. Clarke Predicting the Future in 1964," YouTube video, 3:12, September 8, 2011, *youtube.com.*

RESOURCES

To learn more about Red-Carpet Learning Programs contact us at:
Red-Carpet Learning Worldwide
PO Box 19798
Asheville, NC 28815
www.RedCarpetLearning.com
YouTube: *www.theredcarpetway.tv*
www.RedCarpetLearning.com/EmployeesFirstResources

To download the **2021 What Makes an Employee Feel Valued Report** visit *www.RedCarpetLearning.com/MakeMeFeelValued*

Learn about other experts quoted in Employees First! by visiting their websites:

Christen Rinaldi, LCMHCA – *www.Insight-Owl.com*

Jessica Pettitt, MEd, CSP – *www.GoodEnoughNow.com*

Mike Domitrz – *www.CenterForRespect.com*

Claude Silver – *www.VaynerMedia.com*

Angie Flynn-McIver – *www.IgniteCSP.com*

Rolinda Stotts – *www.BeautifulAsIs.com*

Joseph Fox, EdD, MBA, PHR – *www.foxmgt.com*

Lenora Billings-Harris, CSP, CPAE – *www.UbuntuGlobal.com*

Simone E. Morris – *www.SimoneMorris.com*

Elaine Pasqua, CSP – *www.ElainePasqua.com*

Sadiya Abjani – *www.SageUSA.care*

Denise O'Malley – *www.YouDefineWellness.com*

Lucy Henry – *www.firstsuneap.com*

Krystena Sterling, CPTP, CPC, MA, MS – *www.SterlingCCG.com*

Jason Kotecki – *www.EscapeAdulthood.com*

Karen Maher – *www.WorkplaceTrainwise.com.au*

Dr. Bob Nelson – *www.DrBobNelson.com*

Jeffrey Hayzlett – *www.hayzlett.com*

ACKNOWLEDGMENTS

Sincere gratitude for the many people who have played a role in this labor of love. Here's a list of just a few people who deserve my authentic appreciation.

Readers of my books and people in my audiences, and our Red-Carpet customers. Just by showing up you keep me going!

Jim Cutting, Rolinda Stotts, David Mendes, David Glickman, Lisa Hagan, Lenora Billings-Harris, Christen Rinaldi, and Jessica Pettitt thank you for reading chapters and giving me honest, outstanding feedback. Ron Culberson for coming up with the spot-on subtitle.

Contributors to this book. It has been an absolute honor to tell your stories. You inspire and help many through your example.

Jeffrey Hayzlett for writing the perfect Foreword and for your generous mentorship and encouragement. Kiera Rodriguez for helping to make it all happen. Lisa Hagan for being the best agent an author could ask for, as well as chief encouragement officer and friend. Michael Pye, my editor, and everyone at Red Wheel Weiser for saying YES to *Employees First!* It's a pleasure to work with you.

My cheerleaders Liz Saunders, David Mendes, Kitty Jones, Rolinda Stotts, Christen Rinaldi, Carol Marion Smith, Patricia Bouchard (Mom), and so many other delightful people on and off Facebook.

Finally, to my "pack." Jim Cutting, Moxie and Tonks. The best part of doing anything is doing it with you.

ABOUT THE AUTHOR

Donna Cutting is the founder and CEO of Red-Carpet Learning Worldwide, a consulting firm that helps organizational leaders create cultures of happy people who deliver exceptional service. In addition to *Employees First!* she's the author of two books on customer service: *501 Ways to Roll Out the Red Carpet for Your Customers* and *The Celebrity Experience: Insider Secrets to Delivering Red-Carpet Customer Service.* Named one of the World's Top Customer Service Professionals by Global Gurus (2020, 2021) and Organizational Culture (2021), Donna works with leaders in healthcare, senior living and aging services, education, hospitality, entertainment, call centers, and other fields. Her programs are being used throughout the United States, in Canada, South Africa, and Australia, and her global audience is growing.

An in-demand keynote speaker, Donna has given hundreds of presentations to thousands of people throughout the United States and virtually.

When she's not in Asheville, North Carolina, look for Donna traveling the United States in an RV with her husband, Jim, and their rescue dogs, Moxie and Tonks.